The Amazing Flax Cookbook

by
Jane Reinhardt-Martin, RD, LD

Featuring
Chef Ron Garrett, C.E.C.

Foreword by
JoAnna Lund

The information in this book is intended for general purposes only. While this information can be used to help prevent and treat a wide variety of health problems, realize that certain medical problems and the use of the certain medications may require very specific dietary guildelines. Therefore, the recommendations presented in this book should never replace the sound advice of a qualified medical professional who is familiar with your health history and your health care needs.

Cover design by George Foster, www.fostercovers.com
Interior design by Michael Martin
Cover photography by Newell Commercial Photography, Davenport, IA.
Editing by TSA Press, Moline, IL

Cover pictures are recipes (from top left to bottom right)
Turkey Avocado Wrap
Seafood Topped w/Sauteed Vegetables
Marinara Chicken
Oriental Salad
Coconut Shrimp
Butternut Squash Soup

The Amazing Flax Cookbook
Copyright © 2004 by Jane Reinhardt-Martin

Dedication

To Mike and the boys.
To Rosie and Mary Jo, my sisters, both of whom are inspirational amateur cooks.
And to all those whose drive to self improvement provides an example for us all.

Acknowledgments

First and foremost, I want to thank Ron Garrett, the professional chef whose culinary skills were put to the test as he developed some of the tastiest flax recipes around. Thanks, also to JoAnna Lund, who most graciously agreed to take a peek at my early manuscript. Her creative gifts in sharing healthy, tasty recipes with the world has been an inspiration for me as it has been for her dedicated readers. I am honored that she so kindly agreed to write the foreword for this volume.

This book could never have been produced without the able assistance of my kitchen testers, who dedicated themselves to checking out all the details of each and every recipe, and to ensure that you'll get great results when you try them out in your own home. Diana Garman, Jeannine Gothard, Mickey Schmidt, Andree Connolle, Nicole Eikenberry, Cindy Gay, Stefanie Fila, and Janet Martin, without your dedicated service, rattling those pots and pans, I never could have gotten this project off the ground. And I want to thank my reviewers, Janis Jibrin, Millie Wilson, Nancy Luckenbill, Cathy Leman, Donna Israel, Maggie Green, Shelley Case, and Stephanie Green, who made sure the text was clear and complete.

But perhaps most of all, I want to thank the readers of my first book, *Flax Your Way to Better Health*, for being so responsive to the idea of cooking with flax. So many of you took the trouble to ask for more recipes that you gave me the impetus I needed to produce this book. Your persistence has finally paid off!

Foreword

Many people today are watching what they eat(and cook) for many reasons. Some want to lose weight. Others are choosing healthier alternatives because of health concerns such as diabetes or heart disease. It's great when we can combine both healthy options while still indulging our appreciation for tasty food.

Jane Reinhardt-Martin has done just that in this, her second book featuring flax. She's done both her research and recipe testing. In her first book, *Flax Your Way to Better Health*, she taught us how adding flax to our diet can help fight illness from cancer to heart disease. That's all well and good, but many of us still needed to learn how to easily include flax in recipes that our families will willingly eat. That's just what Jane's newest book helps you do!

In this innovative cookbook you'll find delicious recipes for all occasions, and every one of them features flax in their list of ingredients. If you want a filling soup, try Chicken Noodle Soup with flax noodles, or Butternut Squash Soup topped with toasted flax seed. If you're looking for satisfying main dishes, look no further than Linguini with Shrimp Sauce spotlighting flax linguine, or Mexican Steak and Rice Casserole with ground flaxseed. These are but a few of the many easy recipes that Jane and Chef Ron Garrett have developed to show off the versatility of flax.

I've always said, "It doesn't matter how healthy it is, if it doesn't taste good, who's going to bother?" These recipes deliver both great taste and healthy nutrition. Who could ask for more?

JoAnna M. Lund,
Healthy Exchanges

Introduction

In the fall of 2001 I released my first book on the marvelous nutritional properties and health benefits of flax. That book, *Flax Your Way to Better Health*, met with a public response more gratifying than anything I could have imagined. It seems that there are lots of people out there who are truly curious about finding ways to improve their diets to include more and better foods, and who are hungry for information that will help them make better, healthier, choices. I also discovered that my readers are a communicative bunch—they've been generous in providing me with their feedback. As one reader, Judy, put it, "I'm always looking for new recipes, and the flaxseed bars (featured in *Flax Your Way to Better Health*) were so delicious that I decided to order a copy. I was not disappointed.... I've ordered more copies for friends."

Well, that got me thinking. *Flax Your Way to Better Health* offered a few recipes, but my primary concern in that volume was to explain the benefits of flax, its nutritional composition, and its usefulness in combating specific health problems. My goal was to introduce flax to people who were unfamiliar with it, and to explain why it was worth incorporating it into a healthy diet.

Judy's letter, however, got me to thinking that maybe the time had come to take the next step. Her response was by no means unique—many of my readers have requested recipes, recipes, and more recipes, as well as meal plans and advice about how they might easily incorporate flax into everyday meals. With all that encouragement, I had no choice: I *had* to write this book.

But I wanted to offer something that was really special. I wanted it to offer recipes that met your day-to-day needs, sure—but I also wanted to help you discover the incredible versatility of flax. That meant coming up with inspirational dishes—the kind of foods you'd be proud to serve no matter what the occasion, from everyday meals to holiday feasts. So I decided to consult with experts. My first step was to consult with long-time flax fans, who've been making flax a part of their diet for years.

These people were truly inspirational, providing favorite recipes that have earned rave reviews from their families and friends. They enlightened even me about the myriad of ways that flax can be an integral part of any good cook's repertoire.

Next, I enlisted the help of a true culinary professional. I've known Ron Garrett for years, and I knew him to be a chef of the first caliber. I knew I wanted his expertise, but by the time we really got rolling on this project, it felt like we were fated to work together.

You see, just a few weeks before we were scheduled to sit down together for our first consultation, Ron got something of a shock. An angiogram, done during a regular check-up, revealed that his arteries were seriously clogged. Although they weren't so bad that he had to undergo an immediate angioplasty, their condition suggested that he was facing possible cardiovascular disease in the future. He suddenly realized that if he didn't make some changes in his lifestyle—particularly in his diet—he was looking at a very unpleasant fate.

Those of you who've read my earlier book know that flax has been singled out as a food that demonstrably reduces risk of heart disease. Ron had initially agreed to participate in this project because of our long friendship, but now he had a more personal motivation—he wanted to learn how this flaxseed could help him improve his *own* heart health!

What better kitchen-collaborator could I have asked for? With his skills and training, I knew that Chef Ron would develop delicious recipes that would please the most discriminating of palates. But equally important was his personal commitment—it guaranteed that he'd be working overtime to develop recipes that would maximize the health benefits of cooking with flax. The results, as you'll soon see for yourself, have been nothing short of amazing—Ron had come up with a veritable smorgasbord of recipes that taste great, are easy to make, and make the best possible use of this humble little seed.

In the end, Chef Ron and I had a wonderful time coming up with the recipes in this book, and we hope you have just as much fun trying them out. Even better, we hope you find yourself so inspired by the versatility of flax that you start experimenting on your own. We'd love to hear from you, especially if you've come up with new and creative ways to incorporate flaxseed into your favorite recipes! Who knows? Maybe we'll include one of your creations in future editions of this cookbook, with your name featured in the title!

Table of Contents

Foreword
Introduction

Flax Basics

1

Every good cook knows that there's one thing more important than the latest set of designer cookware or the coolest-looking chef's hat, and that even using a great cookbook isn't enough. Far more important is that you understand the foods you're planning on cooking.

Understanding food is more than knowing how foods interact with each other, and what special qualities or flavors they can impart to the completed dishes. For your health's sake, you need to understand the nutritional value of your foods and what they will contribute to your dietary needs. Flaxseed's unique components have shown potential in the prevention and treatment of heart disease, cancer (breast, prostate, and colon), diabetes, rheumatoid arthritis, kidney disease, constipation, and symptoms of menopause.

So first, let's take a moment to get acquainted with the star of this cookbook, the flaxseed and its derivative, flax oil. Don't worry, I'm not going to overload you with words here. In fact, you'll find most of this information provided in tables—that way you can find the information you need "at a glance." After all, this book is intended as a kitchen resource, not a textbook. For those of you who want the more detailed lowdown, never fear. You can find an in-depth discussion of all these issues in my first book, *Flax Your Way to Better Health*. Ordering information can be found in the back of this book.

Now, let's get down to the nitty gritty about flax!

Calorie Content

Thanks to the recent media blitz, we're all aware of the great American "obesity epidemic." Here's the skinny on the calorie content of a single tablespoon of flax.

Ground Flaxseed (8 grams)	36
Whole Flaxseed (11 grams)	50
Flax Oil (14 grams)	124

Now, I personally feel that obsessing over the number of calories you consume can make you crazy. And simply counting calories is pretty meaningless anyway—it's more important to make sure that the calories you do consume aren't empty! And that's where flax really shows its value, because every one of those calories is packed with nutrients your body needs!

What's In It For Me?

Those tiny flax seeds are just bursting with nutrients you need for good health. In fact, gram-for-gram they're amazingly rich in minerals like phosphorus, magnesium, potassium, calcium, and folic acid. When you add in the fact that they're high in omega-3 fats (more on that later!), their high plant-protein content, and all the good fiber they provide, how can you go wrong? The table below details the nutrient content of a tablespoon of flax, whether ground or whole.

Flaxseed At A Glance		
Nutrient Type	**Ground Seed (8 grams)**	**Whole Seed (11 grams)**
Fat (grams)	3.3	4.5
Protein (grams)	1.6	2.2
Dietary Fiber (grams)	2.2	3.0
Calcium (mg)	18.9	26.0
Magnesium (mg)	34.5	47.4
Phosphorus (mg)	49.8	68.4
Potassium (mg)	66.5	91.4
Folic Acid (mcg)	9.0	12.3

By the way, a tablespoon of flax oil contains 14 grams fat, and no other nutrients. What's important to remember, however, is that the fat in flax oil is high quality—remember those omega-3s?

Oh! Those Omegas

One of the greatest things about flax is that it is one of the richest sources of omega-3 fats in the whole world of plant-derived foods. It may sound funny to hear a food praised for its fat content in these days of high anxiety about fat and cholesterol, but remember: all fats are not created equal! Our bodies need some fats, to absorb fat-soluble vitamins, for example, and for other reasons as well. The point is not to cut out *all* fats, but rather to replace the body-damaging saturated and hydrogenated or "trans" fats with more healthful versions. And one of the healthiest categories of fats are the omega-3s. So let's look at how flax measures up when it comes to fat content.

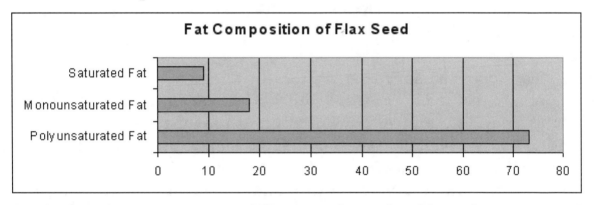

Just look at those percentages! The more heart-healthy polyunsaturated fats make up the largest constituent of flax's fat content, and in that category, the omega-3s are the most plentiful. A single tablespoon of ground flax gives you 1,900 mg of omega-3s, whereas a tablespoon of whole flax offers 2,600 mg, and a tablespoon of flax oil gives you a whopping 8,000 mg of omega-3s! This is great news for people who want to increase their consumption of this healthful nutrient.

To give you an even better idea of how to increase your omega-3 fat intake, check out the meal plans in Chapter 2. Daily omega-3 fat content is listed, as well as the ratio of omega-6 fats and omega-3 fats.

Researchers believe that the current omega-6 fat to omega-3 fat ratio of 20:1 is too high, and is causing numerous health problems. A more healthy ratio that we should aim for is 4:1 average or less. My weekly meal plans are even better with a super-healthful 1:1 ratio.

And while we're on the subject of fats in recipes and meal plans, let's take a minute to discuss a thorny issue. You'll notice that the recipes that follow suggest the use of butter than margarine. This is a question that really puzzles even the professionals in the fields of health and nutrition. So let's just look at the basic facts:

- Butter and margarine provide the same number of calories by volume.
- The calories of both are derived entirely from fat; animal fat in the case of butter, plant fats in the case of margarine.
- Butter is higher in saturated fat than margarine.
- Margarine contains trans-fats, which are just as, or more harmful as saturated fat.

So, where does that leave us? Well, in the end, it is your total intake of fat per day that really matters when it comes to eating healthy. And if you're keeping your fat consumption at reasonable levels, giving priority to the beneficial omegas, the rest is up to personal taste. In the recipes that follow, I call for the use of butter, but I've worked to keep the amounts low, and you are welcome to substitute trans-fat free margarine if that suits your tastes better.

A Few Words About Lignans

Besides omega-3s, flax has another outstanding health benefit that help launch it to nutritional superstardom: lignans. If the word is unfamiliar to you right now, don't be surprised—we've only recently discovered their importance in a healthy diet. Nutritional scientists, however, are rapidly making up for lost time.

Lignans are plant-derived compounds that, when ingested, act like weak versions of the human hormone known as estrogen. These compounds, called phytoestrogens, are extremely beneficial in off-setting the unpleasant physical manifestations of menopause, particularly night sweats and hot flashes. They have also been shown to help in the fight against cancer! And guess what? Flax is the richest known source of lignans in the entire plant kingdom!

Flax Options: Pro and Con

So, now you've got the nutritional basics of flax under your belt, and you've headed off to the grocer or health food store to buy some. Suddenly, you're faced with a choice! Should you buy whole seeds? Ground seeds? Oil? Here's the rundown of each type.

Whole Seed

PRO: Buying whole seeds saves you money, and ensures freshness, so you get the greatest possible nutritional benefit. Two colors to choose from: reddish-brown and golden, both nutritionally the same. The whole seeds stay fresh for one year stored at room temperature. You can easily grind your whole seeds in a coffee grinder or small chopper/grinder when needed. Once ground, place in a tightly-lidded container and store in a cool area, refrigerator, or freezer. Ground seed properly stored can stay fresh for up to four months.

CON: To obtain full nutritional benefit, the seeds need to be ground(or at least the hulls need to be cracked to allow nutrients to escape). Some people have trouble digesting the hard outer coating of whole seeds. If you're troubled by a condition known as diverticulosis, you may experience discomfort or pain from eating whole seeds, because they can get lodged in the intestinal pouches that this malady causes. Just make sure your flaxseed is ground fine, and you should be OK. It's recommended that you should check with your physician before incorporating flax into your diet.

Ground Seed

PRO: Pre-ground flaxseed eliminates the need to do it yourself. A few manufacturers enhance the nutritional quality with extra vitamins and minerals. Very stable in cooking and baking.

CON: There are, as yet, no industry standards for the marketing of ground flaxseed, so getting what you want may be a little confusing. Look for "ground flax" or "milled flaxseed," but check the fat content of "flaxmeal". Some flaxmeals have had some or most of its oil removed. Also, ground seed spoils more quickly than whole seed (shelf life is about four months if kept in a tightly-lidded container).

Flax Oil

PRO: Flax oil is a rich source of alpha-linolenic acid, an omega-3 fat. Flax oil is easy to store in the refrigerator or freezer. Check pressing date and expiration date.

CON: Flax oil contains none of the other nutrients provided by the whole or ground seeds. It is also more expensive than either whole or ground flaxseed. It doesn't keep as well, either. After opened, it keeps for 6 to 8 weeks refrigerated, but if stored at room temperature it must be used within days! It is recommended to be used in cold preparations, should not be used in cooking or baking.

In the recipes that follow, I'll specify whether you need to use whole or ground flaxseed or just flax oil. And for those of you who don't know where to go to buy flax, check out the appendix at the end of the book--you'll find a list of flax manufacturers and retailers, along with their addresses, telephone numbers, and/or internet addresses (for those who like to order online).

Some Final Tips and Tricks

Before you start trying out flax recipes, there are a few final basics you should master if you want to guarantee success:

- Measure ground flax loosely—don't pack it down into a dense mass. Otherwise, your recipe will turn out dry.
- Always level off your measured flax—no heaping spoons-full or overflowing cups.
- Unless the recipe specifically directs you to do otherwise, add your flax at the end of the cooking process. This is especially important in sauces and gravies, because flax has powerful thickening properties and can give your dishes an unpleasant consistency if you add it too early in the cooking process.
- Leftovers should be used within 48 hours or frozen until needed, to preserve optimum taste.

For the more adventurous among you who want to try experimenting with flax on your own, here are a couple of basic rules of substitution:

- When designing bakery recipes, I found that ground flax seemed to act more like a dry ingredient. So, as a general rule, cut down your flour amount by ½ - ¾ cup, and add ½ - ¾ cup ground flax. You will need to experiment with your recipes to obtain optimal taste.
- One tablespoon ground flaxseed + 3 tablespoons water replaces 1 egg. But note that you need to let the flax-water mixture "rest" for a minute or two before using it in a recipe. That way it has a chance to thicken naturally, giving you just the right consistency.

Keep in mind that flaxseed is high in fiber. This means that it will soak up a lot of liquid. To keep your foods moist, you'll want to add extra liquid when you're adapting a traditional recipe to include flax. Add the extra liquid a few drops at a time, to avoid overdoing it.

Finally, there's the perennial problem of post-cooking clean-up. Keep in mind that flax can be pretty tenacious, once you've let it dry! To cut down on scrubbing time, make sure you pop your mixing bowls and cooking pans in for a soak (cold water seems to be more effective) as soon as possible!

Meal Plans 2

In the recipe chapters, you'll discover that flax is amazingly versatile. It lends itself to a wide variety of foods and even beverages! To really expand your use of flax so that it forms a significant part of your everyday eating habits, it sometimes helps to see how individual recipes can fit into your overall meal planning. Here are some meal plans at different calories levels that show you just how easily you can incorporate flax into your life.

The daily meal plan includes the ratio of omega-6 to omega-3 fats. The closer the ratio, the better. You can easily locate this ratio under the Nutrition Information at the bottom of each page.

The
Women's
Slim-Down Flax Diet

For most women, 1500 calories per day combined with a regular exercise program will assist you in losing those unwanted pounds and meeting your quota of omega-3 fats. Feel free to make slight adjustments to meet your needs. If you feel that the calories are too low or too high, we recommend you contact a registered dietitian (RD) in your area to individualize a program just for you. Can't find a RD? Contact the American Dietetic Association at 800/877-1600 or www.eatright.org and click on find nutrition professional.

The Women's Slim-Down Flax Diet
1500 Calorie Meal Plan
WEEK 1

MONDAY

Breakfast	1 cup cooked oatmeal with 1 tablespoon ground flaxseed 1 medium sliced apple & a sprinkle of cinnamon 1 cup skim milk or fat free, calcium enriched soy milk (part w/ oatmeal, rest in cup)
Lunch	Salmon Sandwich - 2 slices whole wheat bread, 3 ounces fresh or canned (no oil) salmon, and 4-5 pieces watercress or other greens ½ cup sliced vegetables of choice 1 cup fruit salad
Snack	90 Calorie light yogurt smoothie or light yogurt
Dinner	1 ½ cups Cassoulet (recipe, page 101) 2 cups tossed spinach salad with 2 tablespoons reduced calorie dressing 1 cup skim milk or fat free, calcium enriched soy milk
Snack	2 medium fig newtons ½ large grapefruit

Nutrition Information
1:2 Ratio

Calories 1520	Fat 26 g	Fiber 41 g
Carbohydrates 242 g	Omega-3 4904 mg	Calcium 1225 mg
Protein 89 g	Cholesterol 90 mg	Sodium 2035 mg

The Women's Slim-Down Flax Diet
1500 Calorie Meal Plan
WEEK 1

T U E S D A Y

Breakfast
½ whole wheat bagel w/ 1 tablespoon low-fat cream cheese
½ large grapefruit
1 cup skim milk or fat free, calcium enriched soy milk

Lunch
Oriental Salad (recipe, page 200)
7 whole wheat crackers (15 calories per cracker)
1 cup skim milk or fat free, calcium enriched soy milk

Snack
90 Calorie light yogurt w/ 1 tablespoon ground flaxseed

Dinner
3 ounces broiled lean hamburger (ground sirloin)
w/ tomato & lettuce on whole wheat bun
1 cup steamed broccoli
1 cup sliced strawberries

Snack
½ ounce or 1/8 cup almonds
Unsweetened green tea (hot or cold)

Nutrition Information
1:1 Ratio

Calories 1505	Fat 62 g	Fiber 27g
Carbohydrates 143 g	Omega-3 7290 mg	Calcium 1385 mg
Protein 104 g	Cholesterol 175 mg	Sodium 1847 mg

The Women's Slim-Down Flax Diet
1500 Calorie Meal Plan
WEEK 1

WEDNESDAY

Breakfast	Banana Berry Supreme (recipe, page 192)
Lunch	Convenience "light" frozen dinner containing chicken, fish or beef w/ rice or pasta & vegetables (up to 300 calories) 2 cups carrot & celery sticks w/ 2 tablespoons reduced calorie dressing 1 cup skim milk or fat free, calcium enriched soy milk
Snack	1 cup tomato or V-8 juice 6 whole wheat crackers (15 calories per cracker)
Dinner	2 cups Chili con Flax (recipe, page 69) 4 saltine crackers 1 cup skim milk or fat free, calcium enriched soy milk
Snack	1 Sugar free frozen fruit bar

Nutrition Information
1:2 Ratio

Calories 1483	Fat 38 g	Fiber 37 g
Carbohydrates 207 g	Omega-3 8437 mg	Calcium 1325 mg
Protein 87 g	Cholesterol 148 mg	Sodium 2910 mg

	The Women's Slim-Down Flax Diet 1500 Calorie Meal Plan WEEK 1

T H U R S D A Y	**Breakfast**	2 whole grain toaster waffles topped with ½ cup low-fat vanilla yogurt & ¾ cup blueberries 1 cup skim milk or fat free, calcium enriched soy milk
	Lunch	PB & Jelly sandwich - 2 slices whole wheat bread, 1 tablespoon peanut butter, and 2 teaspoons jelly 1 cup green & red pepper strips 1 cup skim milk or fat free, calcium enriched soy milk
	Snack	1 cup low-fat cottage cheese w/ 1 tablespoon ground flaxseed ½ cup pineapple
	Dinner	4 ounces lean pork chop, grilled or baked 1 cup cooked wild rice 1 cup steamed mixed vegetables
	Snack	1 small banana rolled in 1 tablespoon ground flaxseed

Nutrition Information 1:1 Ratio

Calories 1512	Fat 38 g	Fiber 22g
Carbohydrates 196 g	Omega-3 4057 mg	Calcium 1281 mg
Protein 103 g	Cholesterol 176 mg	Sodium 1996 mg

The Women's Slim-Down Flax Diet
1500 Calorie Meal Plan
WEEK 1

FRIDAY

Breakfast	1 whole grain english muffin w/ 1-2 teaspoons jelly 1 medium orange 1 cup skim milk or fat free, calcium enriched soy milk
Lunch	90 Calorie light yogurt w/ 1 tablespoon ground flaxseed 1 ½ cups fresh fruit
Snack	1 cup fruit sorbet
Dinner	2 slices Basil & Tomato Pizza (recipe, page 180) 1 cup tossed spinach salad w/ 1 tablespoon reduced calorie salad dressing 1-12 ounce lite beer
Snack	90 Calorie light yogurt smoothie or light yogurt

Nutrition Information
1:2 Ratio

Calories 1520	Fat 33 g	Fiber 23 g
Carbohydrates 237 g	Omega-3 5881 mg	Calcium 1255 mg
Protein 59 g	Cholesterol 95 mg	Sodium 1166 mg

The Women's Slim-Down Flax Diet
1500 Calorie Meal Plan
WEEK 1

SATURDAY

Breakfast	1 slice whole wheat toast w/ 1 teaspoon jelly 1 scrambled egg 1 cup cantaloupe 1 cup skim milk or fat free, calcium enriched soy milk Coffee or tea	
Lunch	T.J.'s Power Drink (recipe, page 197)	
Snack	1 ounce milk or dark chocolate	
Dinner	1 serving Pecan Salmon (recipe, page 149) 1 cup fresh fruit 1 cup steamed asparagus	
Snack	6 cups popped, fat-free popcorn Diet soda of choice	

Nutrition Information
1:2 Ratio

Calories 1497	Fat 58 g	Fiber 29 g
Carbohydrates 168 g	Omega-3 9005 mg	Calcium 934 mg
Protein 88 g	Cholesterol 295 mg	Sodium 973 mg

The Women's Slim-Down Flax Diet
1500 Calorie Meal Plan
WEEK 1

S	**Breakfast**	2 slices french toast - 2 slices whole wheat bread, 1 whole egg, and non-stick skillet Topped with ½ cup fresh fruit & 1 tablespoon ground flax ½ cup orange juice mixed w/ 1 tablespoon ground flax 1 slice lean cooked bacon
U		
N	**Lunch**	1 serving Chicken & Dumplings (recipe, page 140) 1 cup sliced strawberries
D		
A	**Snack**	1 ounce or ¼ cup walnuts
Y		
	Dinner	Turkey salad - 2 cups greens of choice, 2 ounces turkey, ½ cup chopped vegetables of choice, w/ 2 tablespoons reduced calorie salad dressing 4 whole wheat crackers (15 calories per cracker) 1 cup skim milk or fat free, calcium enriched soy milk
	Snack	1 cup cantaloupe

Nutrition Information
2:1 Ratio

Calories 1510	Fat 56 g	Fiber 35 g
Carbohydrates 191 g	Omega-3 8785 mg	Calcium 1397 mg
Protein 78 g	Cholesterol 257 mg	Sodium 2930 mg

The Women's Slim-Down Flax Diet
1500 Calorie Meal Plan
WEEK 2

M O N D A Y

Breakfast	½ medium whole grain bagel w/ 1 tablespoon low-fat cream cheese 1 small banana 1 cup skim milk or fat free, calcium enriched soy milk
Lunch	Chicken sandwich - 2 slices whole wheat bread, 2 ounces roasted chicken (no skin), 1 ounce part-skim mozzarella cheese, 1-2 slices tomato, and greens of choice 1 cup baby carrots 1 medium apple
Snack	1 medium orange 6 whole wheat crackers (15 calories per cracker)
Dinner	1 serving Spaghetti w/ meatballs (recipe, page 88) 1 cup salad (greens of choice) w/ 2 tablespoons reduced calorie salad dressing 1 cup skim milk or fat free, calcium enriched soy milk
Snack	1 slice Pumpkin Date Bread (recipe, page 227)

Nutrition Information
2:1 Ratio

Calories 1516	Fat 44 g	Fiber 28 g
Carbohydrates 210 g	Omega-3 3374 mg	Calcium 1182 mg
Protein 80 g	Cholesterol 193 mg	Sodium 2110 mg

The Women's Slim-Down Flax Diet
1500 Calorie Meal Plan
WEEK 2

T U E S D A Y

Breakfast   1 Banana Chocolate Flax Muffin (recipe, page 230)
1 small tangerine
1 cup skim milk or fat free, calcium enriched soy milk

Lunch   1 vegetable or soy burger w/ whole wheat bun, lettuce,
tomato slice, onion, and catsup/mustard
1 cup fresh fruit
1 cup skim milk or fat free, calcium enriched soy milk

Snack   1 cup low-fat cottage cheese
½ cup mandarin oranges

Dinner   4 ounces broiled whitefish or lake trout
½ cup yams or sweet potatoes
½ cup steamed green beans

Snack   6 cups popped, fat-free popcorn
Diet soda of choice

Nutrition Information
1:2 Ratio

Calories 1520   Fat 32 g   Fiber 26 g
Carbohydrates 208 g   Omega-3 4802 mg   Calcium 998 mg
Protein 107 g   Cholesterol 125 mg Sodium 2020 mg

The Women's Slim-Down Flax Diet
1500 Calorie Meal Plan
WEEK 2

WEDNESDAY

Breakfast	2 slices Pumpkin date bread (recipe, page 227) ½ cup orange juice
Lunch	Salad bar stop - 1 ½ cups greens, ½ cup garbanzo beans, ½ cup broccoli or other chopped vegetables, and 2 tablespoons reduced calorie salad dressing 1 small whole wheat roll 1 cup skim milk or fat free, calcium enriched soy milk
Snack	1 cup tomato or V-8 juice 1 ounce or ¼ cup almonds
Dinner	Grilled Vegetable Sandwich -2 slices whole wheat bread, 1 ounce part-skim mozzarella cheese, 1 teaspoon extra-virgin olive oil, ½ sliced red pepper, 2 onion slices, and 4 tomato slices 1 cup skim milk or fat free, calcium enriched soy milk
Snack	1 small banana rolled in 1 tablespoon ground flaxseed

Nutrition Information
2:1 Ratio

Calories 1507	Fat 56 g	Fiber 30 g
Carbohydrates 200 g	Omega-3 5613 mg	Calcium 1346 mg
Protein 65 g	Cholesterol 141 mg	Sodium 2482 mg

The Women's Slim-Down Flax Diet
1500 Calorie Meal Plan
WEEK 2

THURSDAY

Breakfast	90 Calorie light yogurt w/ 1 tablespoon ground flaxseed 1 cup fresh fruit
Lunch	1 fast food cheeseburger w/ lettuce, tomato, onion, catsup, and mustard Side salad w/ 2 tablespoons reduced calorie salad dressing Diet soda or water
Snack	1 Banana Chocolate Flax Muffin (recipe, page 230) 1 cup skim milk or fat free, calcium enriched soy milk
Dinner	½ breast or 1 leg roasted chicken (remove skin) 1 ½ cups steamed vegetables 1 slice Italian bread
Snack	6 whole wheat crackers (15 calories per cracker) Green tea, unsweetened (hot or cold)

Nutrition Information
1:1 Ratio

Calories 1489	Fat 47 g	Fiber 25 g
Carbohydrates 193 g	Omega-3 4391 mg	Calcium 1155 mg
Protein 82 g	Cholesterol 213 mg	Sodium 1596 mg

The Women's Slim-Down Flax Diet
1500 Calorie Meal Plan
WEEK 2

F R I D A Y

Breakfast	1 cup cooked oatmeal w/ 1 tablespoon ground flaxseed & ¼ cup dried fruit (like cherries or cranberries) 1 cup skim milk or fat free, calcium enriched soy milk (part w/ oatmeal, rest in cup)
Lunch	1 cup low-fat cottage cheese 1 ½ cups fresh fruit 4 whole wheat crackers (15 calories per cracker)
Snack	1 ounce milk or dark chocolate
Dinner	2 slices Vegetarian pizza (recipe, page 182) 1 – 3 ½ ounce glass red or white wine
Snack	1/2 cup fruit sorbet

Nutrition Information
1:2 Ratio

Calories 1495	Fat 37 g	Fiber 22 g
Carbohydrates 213 g	Omega-3 5892 mg	Calcium 882 mg
Protein 69 g	Cholesterol 36 mg	Sodium 2094 mg

The Women's Slim-Down Flax Diet
1500 Calorie Meal Plan
WEEK 2

Breakfast	1 Flax buttermilk pancake (recipe, page 207) 1 cup strawberries 1 cup skim milk or fat free, calcium enriched soy milk	**S A T U R D A Y**
Lunch	Turkey wrap - 7 inch tortilla, 3 ounces skinless turkey, 1 cup vegetables of choice fresh or grilled, and 2 tablespoons salsa 2 cups assorted fresh fruit 1 cup skim milk or fat free, calcium enriched soy milk	
Snack	90 Calorie light yogurt smoothie or light yogurt	
Dinner	1 serving Seafood Topped w/ sautéed vegetables (recipe, page 147) Coffee or tea	
Snack	6 cups popped, fat-free popcorn Diet soda of choice	

Nutrition Information
1:1 Ratio

Calories 1499	Fat 34 g	Fiber 29 g
Carbohydrates 215 g	Omega-3 4032 mg	Calcium 1048 mg
Protein 95 g	Cholesterol 151 mg	Sodium 1366 mg

The Women's Slim-Down Flax Diet
1500 Calorie Meal Plan
WEEK 2

S
U
N
D
A
Y

Breakfast	1 Sticky Cinnamon Roll (recipe, page 211) 1 cup skim milk or fat free, calcium enriched soy milk
Lunch	Grilled cheese sandwich -2 slices whole wheat bread, 1 ½ ounces low-fat cheese, and 1 slice tomato 2 cups fruit salad
Snack	1 Sugar free frozen fruit bar
Dinner	2 cups Bean soup (recipe, page 79) 2 cups greens of choice w/ 2 tablespoons reduced calorie salad dressing 1 cup skim milk or fat free, calcium enriched soy milk
Snack	1 ounce or ¼ cup almonds

Nutrition Information
2:1 Ratio

Calories 1481	Fat 47 g	Fiber 28 g
Carbohydrates 214 g	Omega-3 3690 mg	Calcium 1219 mg
Protein 65 g	Cholesterol 176 mg	Sodium 2108 mg

The Men's Slim-Down Flax Diet

For most men, 1800 calories per day combined with a regular exercise program will assist you in shedding those unwanted pounds and meeting your quota of omega-3 fats. Feel free to make slight adjustments to meet your needs. If you feel that the calories are too low or too high, we recommend you contact a registered dietitian (RD) in your area to individualize a program just for you. Can't find a RD? Contact the American Dietetic Association at 800/877-1600 or www.eatright.org and click on find nutrition professional.

The Men's Slim-Down Flax Diet 1800 Calorie Meal Plan WEEK 1		
M O N D A Y	**Breakfast**	1 cup cooked oatmeal, w/1 tablespoon ground flaxseed, 1 medium sliced apple & a sprinkle of cinnamon 1 cup skim milk or fat free, calcium enriched soy milk (part w/ oatmeal, rest in cup)
	Lunch	Salmon sandwich -2 slices whole wheat bread, 3 ounces fresh or canned (no oil) salmon, and 4-5 pieces watercress or other greens ½ cup sliced vegetables of choice 1 ½ cups fruit salad
	Snack	90 calorie light yogurt smoothie or light yogurt 3 whole wheat crackers
	Dinner	1 ½ cups Cassoulet (recipe, page 101) 2 cups tossed spinach salad with 2 tablespoons reduced calorie dressing 1 cup skim milk or fat free, calcium enriched soy milk
	Snack	4 medium fig newtons 1 large grapefruit
Nutrition Information 1:2 Ratio		

Calories 1805	Fat 30 g	Fiber 46 g
Carbohydrates 305 g	Omega-3 4912 mg	Calcium 1292 mg
Protein 93 g	Cholesterol 90 mg	Sodium 2183 mg

	The Men's Slim-Down Flax Diet 1800 Calorie Meal Plan WEEK 1
T **U** **E** **S** **D** **A** **Y**	**Breakfast** 1 whole wheat bagel w/2 tablespoons low-fat cream cheese ½ large grapefruit 1 cup skim milk or fat free, calcium enriched soy milk
	Lunch Oriental Salad (recipe, page 200) 8 whole wheat crackers (15 calories per cracker) 1 cup skim milk or fat free, calcium enriched soy milk
	Snack 90 Calorie light yogurt with 1 tablespoon ground flaxseed
	Dinner 4 ounces broiled lean hamburger (ground sirloin) with tomato & lettuce on whole wheat bun 1 cup steamed broccoli 1 cup sliced strawberries
	Snack 1 ounce or 1/4 cup almonds Unsweetened green tea(hot or cold)

Nutrition Information
1:1 Ratio

Calories 1785	Fat 78 g	Fiber 32 g
Carbohydrates 165 g	Omega-3 7289 mg	Calcium 1451 mg
Protein 119 g	Cholesterol 207 mg	Sodium 2177 mg

		The Men's Slim-Down Flax Diet 1800 Calorie Meal Plan WEEK 1
W **E** **D** **N** **E** **S** **D** **A** **Y**	**Breakfast**	Banana Berry Supreme (recipe, page 192)
	Lunch	Convenience Light frozen dinner: containing chicken, fish or beef w/ rice or pasta & vegetables (up to 300 calories) 2 cups carrot & celery sticks w/ 2 tablespoons reduced calorie dressing 1 cup fresh fruit (your choice) 1 cup skim milk or fat free, calcium enriched soy milk
	Snack	1 cup tomato or V-8 juice 8 whole wheat crackers (15 calories per cracker)
	Dinner	2 cups Chili con Flax (recipe, page 69) 6 saltine crackers 1 cup fresh fruit (your choice) 1 cup skim milk or fat free, calcium enriched soy milk
	Snack	1 Sugar free frozen fruit bar

Nutrition Information
1:2 Ratio

Calories 1813	Fat 41 g	Fiber 44 g
Carbohydrates 287 g	Omega-3 8437 mg	Calcium 1405 mg
Protein 92 g	Cholesterol 148 mg	Sodium 3012 mg

The Men's Slim-Down Flax Diet
1800 Calorie Meal Plan
WEEK 1

T H U R S D A Y

Breakfast	2 whole grain toaster waffles topped with ½ cup low-fat vanilla yogurt & ¾ cup blueberries 1 cup skim milk or fat free, calcium enriched soy milk
Lunch	PB & Jelly sandwich -2 slices whole wheat bread, 2 tablespoons peanut butter, and 2 teaspoons jelly 1 cup green & red pepper strips ½ cup mandarin oranges 1 cup skim milk or fat free, calcium enriched soy milk
Snack	1 cup low-fat cottage cheese w/ 1 tablespoon ground flaxseed 1 cup pineapple
Dinner	4 ounces lean pork chop, grilled or baked 1 cup cooked wild rice 1 cup steamed mixed vegetables
Snack	1 small banana rolled in 1 tablespoon ground flaxseed

Nutrition Information
2:1 Ratio

Calories 1794	Fat 47 g	Fiber 31 g
Carbohydrates 244 g	Omega-3 4143 mg	Calcium 1346 mg
Protein 112 g	Cholesterol 176 mg	Sodium 2120 mg

The Men's Slim-Down Flax Diet
1800 Calorie Meal Plan
WEEK 1

FRIDAY

Breakfast	1 whole grain english muffin w/ 1 tablespoon peanut butter & 1-2 teaspoons jelly 1 medium orange 1 cup skim milk or fat free, calcium enriched soy milk
Lunch	90 calorie light yogurt w/ 1 tablespoon ground flaxseed 2 cups fresh fruit
Snack	1 cup fruit sorbet
Dinner	2 slices Basil & Tomato Pizza (recipe, page 180) 2 cups tossed spinach salad w/ 2 tablespoons reduced calorie salad dressing 1-12 ounce lite beer
Snack	90 calorie light yogurt smoothie or light yogurt

Nutrition Information
1:1 Ratio

Calories 1800	Fat 46 g	Fiber 27 g
Carbohydrates 271 g	Omega-3 5894 mg	Calcium 1334 mg
Protein 68 g	Cholesterol 155 mg	Sodium 1525 mg

The Men's Slim-Down Flax Diet
1800 Calorie Meal Plan
WEEK 1

SATURDAY

Breakfast
2 slices whole wheat toast   w/ 2 teaspoons jelly
1 scrambled egg
1 cup cantaloupe
1 cup skim milk or fat free, calcium enriched soy milk
Coffee or tea

Lunch
T.J.'s Power Drink (recipe, page 197)

Snack
1 ounce milk or dark chocolate

Dinner
1 serving Pecan Salmon (recipe, page 149)
2 cups fresh fruit
1 ½ cups steamed asparagus

Snack
8 cups popped, fat-free popcorn
Diet soda of choice

Nutrition Information
1:2 Ratio

Calories 1781	Fat 60 g	Fiber 38 g
Carbohydrates 231 g	Omega-3 9015 mg	Calcium 1018 mg
Protein 96 g	Cholesterol 295 mg	Sodium 1115 mg

The Men's Slim-Down Flax Diet
1800 Calorie Meal Plan
WEEK 1

SUNDAY

Breakfast	2 slices french toast - 2 slices whole wheat bread, 1 whole egg, and non-stick skillet Topped with ½ cup fresh fruit & 1 tablespoon ground flax 1 slice lean cooked bacon ½ cup orange juice mixed w/ 1 tablespoon ground flax
Lunch	1 serving Chicken & Dumplings (recipe, page 140) 2 cups sliced strawberries
Snack	2 ounces or ½ cup walnuts
Dinner	Turkey salad - 2 cups greens of choice, 3 ounces turkey, ½ cup chopped vegetables of choice, w/ 2 tablespoons reduced calorie salad dressing 6 whole wheat crackers (15 calories per cracker) 1 cup skim milk or fat free, calcium enriched soy milk
Snack	1 cup cantaloupe

Nutrition Information
2:1 Ratio

Calories 1801	Fat 76 g	Fiber 41 g
Carbohydrates 214 g	Omega-3 11,500 mg	Calcium 1453 mg
Protein 88 g	Cholesterol 266 mg	Sodium 3314 mg

The Men's Slim-Down Flax Diet
1800 Calorie Meal Plan
WEEK 2

Breakfast	1 medium whole grain bagel w/ 2 tablespoons low-fat cream cheese 1 small banana 1 cup skim milk or fat free, calcium enriched soy milk
Lunch	Chicken sandwich - 2 slices whole wheat bread, 3 ounces roasted chicken (no skin), 1 ounce part-skim mozzarella cheese, 1-2 slices tomato, and greens of choice 1 cup baby carrots 1 medium apple
Snack	2 medium oranges 8 whole wheat crackers (15 calories per cracker)
Dinner	1 serving Spaghetti w/ meatballs (recipe, page 88) 1 ½ cups salad (greens of choice) w/ 2 tablespoons reduced calorie salad dressing 1 cup skim milk or fat free, calcium enriched soy milk
Snack	1 slice Pumpkin Date Bread (recipe, page 227)

MONDAY

Nutrition Information
2:1 Ratio

Calories 1812	Fat 53 g	Fiber 36 g
Carbohydrates 253 g	Omega-3 3423 mg	Calcium 1298 mg
Protein 95 g	Cholesterol 253 mg	Sodium 2432 mg

The Men's Slim-Down Flax Diet
1800 Calorie Meal Plan
WEEK 2

TUESDAY

Breakfast	1 Banana Chocolate Flax Muffin (recipe, page 230) 1 small tangerine 1 cup skim milk or fat free, calcium enriched soy milk
Lunch	1 vegetable or soy burger w/ whole wheat bun, lettuce, tomato slice, onion, and catsup/mustard 1 ounce potato chips 1 cup fresh fruit 1 cup skim milk or fat free, calcium enriched soy milk
Snack	1 cup low-fat cottage cheese ½ cup mandarin oranges
Dinner	4 ounces broiled whitefish or lake trout 1 cup yams or sweet potatoes 1 cup steamed green beans
Snack	6 cups popped, fat-free popcorn Diet soda of choice

Nutrition Information
1:1 Ratio

Calories 1811	Fat 44 g	Fiber 32 g
Carbohydrates 249 g	Omega-3 4840 mg	Calcium 1061 mg
Protein 112 g	Cholesterol 125 mg	Sodium 2209 mg

The Men's Slim-Down Flax Diet
1800 Calorie Meal Plan
WEEK 2

WEDNESDAY

Breakfast
2 slices Pumpkin date bread (recipe, page 227)
1cup orange juice

Lunch
Salad bar stop - 2 cups greens, 2/3 cup garbanzo beans,
¾ cup broccoli or other chopped vegetables, and 2
tablespoons reduced calorie salad dressing
2 small whole wheat rolls
1 cup skim milk or fat free, calcium enriched soy milk

Snack
1 cup tomato or V-8 juice
1 ounce or ¼ cup almonds

Dinner
Grilled Vegetable Sandwich -2 slices whole wheat bread,
2 ounces part-skim mozzarella cheese, 1 teaspoon extra-
virgin olive oil, ½ sliced red pepper, 2 onion slices, and 4
tomato slices
1 cup skim milk or fat free, calcium enriched soy milk

Snack
1 small banana rolled in 1 tablespoon ground flaxseed

Nutrition Information
2:1 Ratio

Calories 1792
Carbohydrates 239 g
Protein 80 g

Fat 65 g
Omega-3 5675 mg
Cholesterol 188 mg

Fiber 35 g
Calcium 1751 mg
Sodium 2836 mg

The Men's Slim-Down Flax Diet
1800 Calorie Meal Plan
WEEK 2

THURSDAY

Breakfast	90 Calorie light yogurt w/ 1 tablespoon ground flaxseed 1 cup fresh fruit
Lunch	1 fast food cheeseburger w/ lettuce, tomato, onion, catsup, and mustard Side salad w/ 2 tablespoons reduced calorie salad dressing Diet soda or water
Snack	1 Banana chocolate flax muffin (recipe, page 230) 1 cup skim milk or fat free, calcium enriched soy milk
Dinner	½ breast or 1 leg roasted chicken (remove skin) 2 cups steamed vegetables 1 slice Italian bread w/ 1 teaspoon olive oil 1 cup fresh fruit
Snack	10 whole wheat crackers (15 calories per cracker) Green tea, unsweetened (hot or cold)

Nutrition Information
1:1 Ratio

Calories 1785	Fat 54 g	Fiber 33 g
Carbohydrates 251 g	Omega-3 4435 mg	Calcium 1220 mg
Protein 88 g	Cholesterol 213 mg	Sodium 1718 mg

The Men's Slim-Down Flax Diet
1800 Calorie Meal Plan
WEEK 2

Breakfast
1 cup cooked oatmeal w/ 1 tablespoon ground flaxseed & ½ cup dried fruit (like cherries or cranberries)
1 cup skim milk or fat free, calcium enriched soy milk (part w/ oatmeal, rest in cup)

Lunch
1 cup low-fat cottage cheese
2 cups fresh fruit
6 whole wheat crackers (15 calories per cracker)

Snack
1 ounce milk or dark chocolate

Dinner
2 slices Vegetarian pizza (recipe, page 182)
1 – 3 ½ ounce glass red or white wine

Snack
1 cup fruit sorbet

FRIDAY

Nutrition Information
1:2 Ratio

Calories 1806	Fat 38 g	Fiber 25 g
Carbohydrates 291 g	Omega-3 5906 mg	Calcium 927 mg
Protein 72 g	Cholesterol 36 mg	Sodium 2157 mg

The Men's Slim-Down Flax Diet
1800 Calorie Meal Plan
WEEK 2

SATURDAY

Breakfast	2 Flax buttermilk pancakes (recipe, page 207) 2 cups strawberries 1 cup skim milk or fat free, calcium enriched soy milk
Lunch	Turkey wrap - 7 inch tortilla, 3 ounces turkey, 1 cup vegetables of choice fresh or grilled, and 2 tablespoons salsa 2 cups assorted fresh fruit 1 cup skim milk or fat free, calcium enriched soy milk
Snack	90 calorie light yogurt smoothie or light yogurt 6 whole wheat crackers
Dinner	1 serving Seafood Topped w/ sautéed vegetables (recipe, page 147) Coffee or tea
Snack	8 cups popped, fat-free popcorn Diet soda of choice

Nutrition Information
1:1 Ratio

Calories 1820	Fat 43 g	Fiber 40 g
Carbohydrates 270 g	Omega-3 5313 mg	Calcium 1200 mg
Protein 104 g	Cholesterol 179 mg	Sodium 1905 mg

The Men's Slim-Down Flax Diet
1800 Calorie Meal Plan
WEEK 2

Breakfast
1 Sticky Cinnamon Roll (recipe, page 211)
1 medium orange
1 cup skim milk or fat free, calcium enriched soy milk

Lunch
Grilled cheese sandwich- 2 slices whole wheat bread,
3 ounces low-fat cheese, and 1 slices tomato
2 cups fruit salad

Snack
1 Sugar free frozen fruit bar

Dinner
2 cups Bean soup (recipe, page 79)
2 cups greens of choice w/ 2 tablespoons reduced calorie salad dressing
1 cup skim milk or fat free, calcium enriched soy milk

Snack
2 ounces or ½ cup almonds

SUNDAY

Nutrition Information
3:1 Ratio

Calories 1788	Fat 65 g	Fiber 34 g
Carbohydrates 236 g	Omega-3 3734 mg	Calcium 1532 mg
Protein 82 g	Cholesterol 185 mg	Sodium 2465 mg

The Athlete's Flax Diet

Most athletes will need more calories than our other plans. Some athletes, may require more calories than this meal plan, so you may need to adjust your meals and snacks accordingly. Need help making those adjustments? We recommend you contact a registered dietitian (RD) in your area to individualize this program just for you. Can't find a RD? Contact the American Dietetic Association at 800/877-1600 or www.eatright.org and click on find nutrition professional.

M O N D A Y	The Athlete's Flax Diet 2200 Calorie Meal Plan WEEK 1	

Breakfast	2 cups cooked oatmeal with 1 tablespoon ground flaxseed 1 medium sliced apple & a sprinkle of cinnamon 1 cup skim milk or fat free, calcium enriched soy milk (part w/ oatmeal, rest in cup)
Lunch	Salmon sandwich -2 slices whole wheat bread, 3 ounces fresh or canned (no oil) salmon, and 4-5 pieces watercress or other greens ½ cup sliced vegetables of choice 2 cups fruit salad
Snack	90 Calorie light yogurt smoothie or light yogurt 6 whole wheat crackers
Dinner	2 cups Cassoulet (recipe, page 101) 2 cups tossed spinach salad with 2 tablespoons reduced calorie dressing 1 cup skim milk or fat free, calcium enriched soy milk
Snack	4 medium fig newtons 1 large grapefruit

Nutrition Information
1:1 Ratio

Calories 2206	Fat 37 g	Fiber 60 g
Carbohydrates 375 g	Omega-3 5967 mg	Calcium 1395 mg
Protein 111 g	Cholesterol 101 mg	Sodium 2442 mg

The Athlete's Flax Diet 2200 Calorie Meal Plan WEEK 1

T U E S D A Y	**Breakfast**	1 whole wheat bagel w/2 tablespoons low-fat cream cheese 1 large grapefruit 1 cup skim milk or fat free, calcium enriched soy milk
	Lunch	Oriental Salad (recipe, page 200) 8 whole wheat crackers (15 calories per cracker) 1 cup skim milk or fat free, calcium enriched soy milk
	Snack	90 Calorie light yogurt w/ 1 tablespoon ground flaxseed 8 whole wheat crackers (15 calories per cracker)
	Dinner	5 ounces broiled lean hamburger (ground sirloin) with tomato & lettuce on whole wheat bun 2 cups steamed broccoli 2 cups sliced strawberries 1 cup skim milk or fat free, calcium enriched soy milk
	Snack	1 ounce or 1/4 cup almonds Unsweetened green tea (hot or cold)

Nutrition Information 1:1 Ratio

Calories 2213	Fat 89 g	Fiber 45 g
Carbohydrates 230 g	Omega-3 7430 mg	Calcium 1885 mg
Protein 144 g	Cholesterol 235 mg	Sodium 2613 mg

The Athlete's Flax Diet	

The Athlete's Flax Diet
2200 Calorie Meal Plan
WEEK 1

W E D N E S D A Y

Breakfast Banana Berry Supreme (recipe, page 192)

Lunch Convenience light frozen dinner containing chicken, fish or beef w/ rice or pasta & vegetables (up to 400 calories)
2 cups carrot & celery sticks w/ 2 tablespoons reduced calorie dressing
1 cup fresh fruit (your choice)
1 cup skim milk or fat free, calcium enriched soy milk

Snack 1 cup tomato or V-8 juice
12 whole wheat crackers (15 calories per cracker)

Dinner 2 cups Chili con Flax (recipe, page 69)
10 saltine crackers
2 cups fresh fruit (your choice)
1 cup skim milk or fat free, calcium enriched soy milk

Snack 1 sugar free frozen fruit bar

Nutrition Information
1:2 Ratio

Calories 2186	Fat 49 g	Fiber 49 g
Carbohydrates 349 g	Omega-3 8437 mg	Calcium 1495 mg
Protein 105 g	Cholesterol 200 mg	Sodium 4194 mg

The Athlete's Flax Diet
2200 Calorie Meal Plan
WEEK 1

T H U R S D A Y

Breakfast	2 whole grain toaster waffles topped with ½ cup low-fat vanilla yogurt & ¾ cup blueberries 1 cup skim milk or fat free, calcium enriched soy milk
Lunch	PB & Jelly sandwich- 2 slices whole wheat bread, 2 tablespoons peanut butter, and 2 teaspoons jelly 2 cups green & red pepper strips 1 cup mandarin oranges 1 cup skim milk or fat free, calcium enriched soy milk
Snack	1 cup low-fat cottage cheese w/ 1 tablespoon ground flaxseed 1 cup pineapple
Dinner	4 ounces lean pork chop, grilled or baked 1 ½ cups cooked wild rice 2 cups steamed mixed vegetables
Snack	1 large banana rolled in 2 tablespoons ground flaxseed

Nutrition Information
1:1 Ratio

Calories 2180	Fat 52 g	Fiber 46 g
Carbohydrates 325 g	Omega-3 6108 mg	Calcium 1447 mg
Protein 122 g	Cholesterol 176 mg	Sodium 2191 mg

The Athlete's Flax Diet
2200 Calorie Meal Plan
WEEK 1

F R I D A Y

Breakfast	1 whole grain english muffin w/ 1 tablespoon peanut butter & 1-2 teaspoons jelly 1 medium orange 1 cup skim milk or fat free, calcium enriched soy milk
Lunch	90 Calorie light yogurt w/ 1 tablespoon ground flaxseed 1 whole wheat bagel 2 cups fresh fruit
Snack	1 cup fruit sorbet 4 whole wheat crackers (15 calories per cracker)
Dinner	3 slices Basil & Tomato Pizza (recipe, page 180) 2 cups tossed spinach salad w/ 2 tablespoons reduced calorie salad dressing 1-12 ounce lite beer
Snack	90 Calorie light yogurt smoothie or light yogurt

Nutrition Information
1:1 Ratio

Calories 2205	Fat 59 g	Fiber 38g
Carbohydrates 330 g	Omega-3 8025 mg	Calcium 1488 mg
Protein 85 g	Cholesterol 163 mg	Sodium 2041 mg

The Athlete's Flax Diet
2200 Calorie Meal Plan
WEEK 1

S A T U R D A Y

Breakfast	2 slices whole wheat toast w/ 2 teaspoons jelly 1 scrambled egg 2 cups cantaloupe 1 cup skim milk or fat free, calcium enriched soy milk Coffee or tea
Lunch	T.J.'s Power Drink (recipe, page 197)
Snack	2 ounces milk or dark chocolate
Dinner	1 serving Pecan Salmon (recipe, page 149) 1 cup wild rice 2 cups fresh fruit 2 cups steamed asparagus
Snack	8 cups popped, fat-free popcorn Diet soda of choice

Nutrition Information
1:2 Ratio

Calories 2219	Fat 71 g	Fiber 45 g
Carbohydrates 310 g	Omega-3 9171 mg	Calcium 1127 mg
Protein 107 g	Cholesterol 300 mg	Sodium 1164 mg

The Athlete's Flax Diet
2200 Calorie Meal Plan
WEEK 1

SUNDAY

Breakfast	2 slices french toast -2 slices whole wheat bread, 1 whole egg, and non-stick skillet Topped with ½ cup fresh fruit & 1 tablespoon ground flax 1 slice lean cooked bacon 1 cup orange juice mixed w/ 1 tablespoon ground flax
Lunch	1 serving Chicken & Dumplings (recipe, page 140) 2 cups sliced strawberries 1 cup skim milk or fat free, calcium enriched soy milk
Snack	2 ounces or ½ cup walnuts 2 medium apples
Dinner	Turkey salad - 2 cups greens of choice, 4 ounces turkey, 1 cup chopped vegetables of choice, w/ 2 tablespoons reduced calorie salad dressing 10 whole wheat crackers (15 calories per cracker) 1 cup skim milk or fat free, calcium enriched soy milk
Snack	1 cup cantaloupe

Nutrition Information
2:1 Ratio

Calories 2190	Fat 80 g	Fiber 50 g
Carbohydrates 291 g	Omega-3 11,600 mg	Calcium 1943 mg
Protein 104 g	Cholesterol 280 mg	Sodium 3880 mg

The Athlete's Flax Diet
2200 Calorie Meal Plan
WEEK 2

MONDAY

Breakfast	1 medium whole grain bagel w/ 2 tablespoons low-fat cream cheese 1 large banana 1 cup skim milk or fat free, calcium enriched soy milk
Lunch	Chicken sandwich - 2 slices whole wheat bread, 3 ounces roasted chicken (no skin), 1 ounce part-skim mozzarella cheese, 1-2 slices tomato, and greens of choice 1 cup baby carrots 1 medium apple
Snack	2 medium oranges 10 whole wheat crackers (15 calories per cracker)
Dinner	1 serving Spaghetti w/ meatballs (recipe, page 88) 1 slice Italian bread with 1 teaspoon extra-virgin olive oil 2 cups salad (greens of choice) w/ 3 tablespoons reduced calorie salad dressing 1 cup skim milk or fat free, calcium enriched soy milk
Snack	2 slices Pumpkin Date Bread (recipe, page 227)

Nutrition Information
1:1 Ratio

Calories 2174	Fat 69 g	Fiber 42 g
Carbohydrates 301 g	Omega-3 5223 mg	Calcium 1377 mg
Protein 103 g	Cholesterol 295 mg	Sodium 2946 mg

The Athlete's Flax Diet
2200 Calorie Meal Plan
WEEK 2

Breakfast	2 Banana Chocolate Flax Muffins (recipe, page 230) 1 small tangerine 1 cup skim milk or fat free, calcium enriched soy milk	**T U E S D A Y**
Lunch	1 vegetable or soy burger w/ whole wheat bun, lettuce, tomato slice, onion, and catsup/mustard 1 ounce potato chips 1 cup fresh fruit 1 cup skim milk or fat free, calcium enriched soy milk	
Snack	1 cup low-fat cottage cheese 1 cup mandarin oranges	
Dinner	6 ounces broiled whitefish or lake trout 1 cup yams or sweet potatoes 1 cup steamed green beans	
Snack	6 cups popped, fat-free popcorn Diet soda of choice	

Nutrition Information
1:1 Ratio

Calories 2185	Fat 59 g	Fiber 36 g
Carbohydrates 292 g	Omega-3 8463 mg	Calcium 1125 mg
Protein 131 g	Cholesterol 189 mg	Sodium 2371 mg

The Athlete's Flax Diet 2200 Calorie Meal Plan WEEK 2	
Breakfast	2 slices Pumpkin date bread (recipe, page 227) 1 cup orange juice
Lunch	Salad bar stop - 2 cups greens, 2 ounces turkey (no skin), 1 cup garbanzo beans, ¾ cup broccoli or other chopped vegetables, and 2 tablespoons reduced calorie salad dressing 2 small whole wheat rolls 1 cup skim milk or fat free, calcium enriched soy milk
Snack	1 cup tomato or V-8 juice 2 ounces or ½ cup almonds
Dinner	Grilled Vegetable Sandwich -2 slices whole wheat bread, 2 ounces part-skim mozzarella cheese, 1 teaspoon extra-virgin olive oil, ½ sliced red pepper, 2 onion slices, and 4 tomato slices 1 cup skim milk or fat free, calcium enriched soy milk
Snack	1 large banana rolled in 1 tablespoon ground flaxseed

WEDNESDAY

Nutrition Information
2:1 Ratio

Calories 2186	Fat 83 g	Fiber 43 g
Carbohydrates 270 g	Omega-3 5726 mg	Calcium 1867 mg
Protein 109 g	Cholesterol 227 mg	Sodium 2874 mg

The Athlete's Flax Diet
2200 Calorie Meal Plan
WEEK 2

THURSDAY

Breakfast
90 Calorie light yogurt w/ 1 tablespoon ground flaxseed
2 cups fresh fruit

Lunch
1 fast food cheeseburger w/ lettuce, tomato, onion, catsup, and mustard
1 small order French fries
Side salad w/ 2 tablespoons reduced calorie salad dressing
Diet soda or water

Snack
1 Banana Chocolate Flax Muffin (recipe, page 230)
1 cup skim milk or fat free, calcium enriched soy milk

Dinner
1 breast or 2 legs roasted chicken (remove skin)
2 cups steamed vegetables
1 slice Italian bread w/ 1 teaspoon olive oil
1 cup fresh fruit

Snack
10 whole wheat crackers (15 calories per cracker)
Green tea, unsweetened (hot or cold)

Nutrition Information
1:1 Ratio

Calories 2220	Fat 69 g	Fiber 37 g
Carbohydrates 312 g	Omega-3 4475 mg	Calcium 1276 mg
Protein 108 g	Cholesterol 265 mg	Sodium 1860 mg

The Athlete's Flax Diet
2200 Calorie Meal Plan
WEEK 2

FRIDAY

Breakfast	2 cups cooked oatmeal w/ 1 tablespoon ground flaxseed & ½ cup dried fruit (like cherries or cranberries) 1 cup skim milk or fat free, calcium enriched soy milk (part w/ oatmeal, rest in cup)
Lunch	1 cup low-fat cottage cheese 2 cups fresh fruit 10 whole wheat crackers (15 calories per cracker)
Snack	1 ounce milk or dark chocolate
Dinner	3 slices Vegetarian pizza (recipe, page 182) 1 – 3 ½ ounce glass red or white wine
Snack	1 cup fruit sorbet

Nutrition Information
1:2 Ratio

Calories 2207	Fat 52 g	Fiber 36g
Carbohydrates 346 g	Omega-3 7960 mg	Calcium 1088 mg
Protein 89 g	Cholesterol 44 mg	Sodium 2887 mg

	The Athlete's Flax Diet 2200 Calorie Meal Plan WEEK 2
Breakfast	3 Flax Buttermilk Pancakes (recipe, page 207) 2 cups strawberries 1 cup skim milk or fat free, calcium enriched soy milk
Lunch	Turkey wrap- 10 inch tortilla, 4 ounces turkey, 1 cup vegetables of choice fresh or grilled, and ¼ cup salsa 2 cups assorted fresh fruit 1 cup skim milk or fat free, calcium enriched soy milk
Snack	90 Calorie light yogurt smoothie or light yogurt 8 whole wheat crackers
Dinner	1 serving Seafood Topped w/ sautéed vegetables (recipe, page 147; use 6 ounces fish) Coffee or tea
Snack	8 cups popped, fat-free popcorn Diet soda of choice

SATURDAY

Nutrition Information
1:1 Ratio

Calories 2189	Fat 58 g	Fiber 45 g
Carbohydrates 303 g	Omega-3 6521 mg	Calcium 1369 mg
Protein 131 g	Cholesterol 254 mg	Sodium 2550 mg

The Athlete's Flax Diet
2200 Calorie Meal Plan
WEEK 2

Breakfast	2 Sticky Cinnamon Rolls (recipe, page 211) 2 medium oranges 1 cup skim milk or fat free, calcium enriched soy milk
Lunch	Grilled cheese sandwich - 2 slices whole wheat bread, 3 ounces low-fat cheese, and 1 slices tomato 2 cups fruit salad
Snack	1 Sugar free frozen fruit bar
Dinner	2 cups Bean soup (recipe, page 79) 6 saltine crackers 2 cups greens of choice w/ 2 tablespoons reduced calorie salad dressing 1 cup skim milk or fat free, calcium enriched soy milk
Snack	2 ounces or ½ cup almonds

SUNDAY

Nutrition Information
2:1 Ratio

Calories 2188	Fat 76 g	Fiber 41 g
Carbohydrates 306 g	Omega-3 5952 mg	Calcium 1641 mg
Protein 90 g	Cholesterol 224 mg	Sodium 2679 mg

Some Kitchen Essentials 3

Flaxseed and flax oil are, of course, great to use as an integral part of recipes, and most of the chapters ahead will deal with them in just that context. But because of its form, flax is equally useful in toppings, spreads, and breadings. Here are some great ways to add a little of that ol' flax magic to these culinary "extras."

Toasted Flax

Nothing beats the warm, nutty flavor of toasted flax. You can use it as a garnish on soups, stews, or chowders, or as a topping for casseroles. It makes a tasty dessert topping, too. You can sprinkle it over ice cream, or you can dip fresh fruit in it—it's the perfect flavor complement for bananas, strawberries, kiwis, and apples. Best of all, toasting flax seed is as simple as 1-2-3!

1. Place whole (not ground) flaxseed into a small flat pan with a long handle, and cover securely.

2. Hold pan over high heat, shaking it vigorously to keep the seeds from burning. In moments, you'll hear the flaxseed start to pop—just like popcorn!

3. As soon as the popping stops (it only takes a few minutes), immediately remove the pan from the heat and remove the cover.

Voila! Your toasted flaxseed will look darker in color, and the hulls will have split. Toasting gives flax a richer, nuttier flavor and a crunchy texture. Best of all, the toasted version doesn't get stuck in your teeth the way the raw seeds do.

You may be wondering if toasting will rob your flaxseed of its nutritional value (especially the Omega-3s). Very little of the Omega-3 fats are lost during the toasting process. I asked Nancy Kangas, research specialist for the Agricultural and Biosystems Department at North Dakota State University to run some tests for us, and she gave us some practical news. She tells us that when you start with a good quality seed, your toasted flaxseed, stored in an airtight container in the fridge, can stay fresh for at least two weeks!

Breadings

All good cooks know the value of breading. It helps meat retain its juices while adding flavor and texture. Breadings are simplicity itself—just combine the dry ingredients in a bowl, stir thoroughly, and they're ready to use. All the variations appearing below can be stored for up to 2 weeks in the fridge, as long as you keep them in airtight containers. But, when fresh herbs are used, you'll want to use them right away for optimal flavor.

Breading your food is a three stage process (unless noted). First, coat your food with seasoned flour, then dip in egg wash, and lastly apply the breading.

Seasoned Flour	**Egg Wash**
Preparation time: 3 minutes	*Preparation time: 3 minutes*
Yield: ½ cup	*Yield: ½ cup*
1/2 cup all purpose flour	1 egg, beaten
1/2 teaspoon black pepper	1/4 cup skim milk
1/8 teaspoon garlic powder	
salt to taste	

Basic Flax Breading

Preparation time: 3 minutes
Yield: 1 1/4 cups
Suggested foods: chicken, pork,
veal, beef, turkey

1/2 cup plain bread crumbs
1/2 cup ground flaxseed
1/4 teaspoon garlic powder
1/2 teaspoon black pepper
1 tablespoon dried parsley flakes
or fresh chopped parsley
1 tablespoon grated Parmesan
cheese
1/4 teaspoon Italian seasoning
 salt, to taste

Walnut Flax Breading

Preparation time: 5 minutes
Yield: 1 1/3 cups
Suggested foods: chicken, salmon,
red fish, catfish, pork, turkey

1/2 cup plain bread crumbs
1/2 cup ground flaxseed
1/8 teaspoon leaf rosemary or
fresh chopped rosemary
1/2 teaspoon black pepper
1 tablespoon dried parsley flakes
or fresh chopped parsley
1/4 cup walnuts, chopped finely
 salt, to taste

Pecan Flax Breading

Preparation time: 5 minutes
Yield: 1 1/3 cups
Suggested foods: chicken, salmon,
red fish, catfish, pork, turkey

1/2 cup plain bread crumbs
1/2 cup ground flaxseed
1/4 teaspoon garlic powder
1/2 teaspoon black pepper
1 tablespoon dried parsley flakes
or fresh chopped parsley
1/4 cup pecans, chopped finely
 salt, to taste

Southwestern Flax Breading

Preparation time: 3 minutes
Yield: 1 1/3 cups
Suggested foods: chicken, pork,
beef, catfish, turkey, redfish

1/2 cup plain bread crumbs
1/2 cup ground flaxseed
1/4 teaspoon garlic powder
1/2 teaspoon black pepper
1 tablespoon dried parsley flakes
or fresh chopped parsley
1 tablespoon chili powder
1/2 teaspoon cumin
1-1/2 teaspoons cilantro or fresh
chopped cilantro
2 tablespoons dried minced
onions
salt, to taste

Almond Flax Breading
Preparation time: 5 minutes
Yield: 1 1/3 cups
Suggested foods: chicken, salmon,
red fish, catfish, pork, turkey, sole

1/2 cup plain bread crumbs
1/2 cup ground flaxseed
1/8 teaspoon ground mustard
1/8 teaspoon ground ginger
1/2 teaspoon black pepper
1-1/2 teaspoons white sugar
1 tablespoon dried parsley flakes
or fresh chopped parsley
1/4 cup almonds, chopped finely
salt, to taste

Horseradish Flax Crust
Preparation time: 3 minutes
Yield: 1 ¼ cups
Suggested foods:
Beef(particularly steak), pork,
turkey
Special note: this is a crust, not a
breading. Normally goes on the top
only, and finished in a broiler or hot
oven until lightly browned;
do not use egg wash and flour

½ cup plain bread crumbs
¼ cup ground flaxseed
½ cup prepared horseradish
4 tablespoons unsalted butter,
melted or ¼ cup extra-virgin
olive oil
½ teaspoon black pepper
salt, to taste

Asian Flax Breading
Preparation time: 3 minutes
Yield: 1 1/3 cups
Suggested foods: chicken, veal,
pork, beef, shrimp, salmon

1/2 cup plain bread crumbs
1/2 cup ground flaxseed
1/8 teaspoon ground mustard
1/8 teaspoon ground ginger
1/2 teaspoon white pepper
1-1/2 teaspoons white sugar
1 tablespoon dried parsley flakes
or fresh chopped parsley
1/8 cup sesame seeds
salt, to taste

My boys love this breading for "chicken
nuggets"! I use fresh boneless, skinless
chicken breasts cut in strips, dredge
them in flour and dip in an egg wash,
then coat the nuggets in the breading
prior to cooking.

Coconut Flax Breading
Preparation time: 3 minutes
Yield: 1 1/4 cups total
Suggested foods: chicken

1/2 cup shredded coconut
1/2 cup bread crumbs, oriental
style or panko
1/4 cup ground flaxseed

Cajun Flax Coating

Preparation time: 3 minutes
Yield: 1 cup total
Suggested foods: chicken, veal, beef, pork, catfish, turkey, redfish, shrimp

Note: used as a seasoning and doesn't require the use of seasoned flour or an egg wash

2 tablespoons paprika
1/2 cup ground flaxseed
1 tablespoon black pepper
1/2 teaspoon ground cumin
1/2 teaspoon cayenne pepper
1/2 teaspoon ground oregano
1/2 teaspoon ground thyme
1/2 teaspoon basil
 seasoned salt, to taste

Cajun Flax Breading

Preparation time: 5 minutes
Yield: 2 cups
Suggested foods: chicken, veal, beef, pork, catfish, turkey, redfish, shrimp

1 cup bread crumbs
3/4 cup ground flaxseed
1 tablespoon paprika
1 teaspoon black pepper
2 teaspoons cayenne pepper
1 tablespoon Italian Blend
 salt, to taste
1/4 cup dried parsley flakes or fresh chopped parsley

This recipe comes courtesy of Andree Connolle, R.D., of New Orleans. A southern gal, born and bred, she loves those Cajun spices!

Salt Free Seasonings

If you're watching your sodium intake, but you don't want to resign yourself to bland, unseasoned foods, flaxseed combines wonderfully well with herbs and spices to make a no-salt alternative. Here are some great blended seasonings for you to make. Just combine the ingredients in a bowl, then decant the mixture into your own spice bottles. They also make thoughtful gifts for your culinarily inclined friends!

Herb Blend

1-1/2 teaspoons ground sage
1 tablespoon ground thyme
1 tablespoon ground marjoram
2-1/2 teaspoons leaf rosemary
2 tablespoons ground flaxseed

Mediterranean Blend

1 tablespoon dried dill weed or
leaf basil or dried mint leaf
1 tablespoon onion powder
1/2 teaspoon leaf oregano
1/2 teaspoon celery seed
1/4 teaspoon dried lemon peel
1/8 teaspoon black pepper
2 tablespoons ground flaxseed
1/8 teaspoon allspice(optional)

Spicy Seasoning

1 tablespoon savory*
1/2 tablespoon ground mustard
1 teaspoon onion powder
1/2 teaspoon curry powder
1/2 teaspoon white pepper
1/2 teaspoon ground cumin
1/4 teaspoon garlic powder
2 tablespoons ground flaxseed

*or 1 teaspoon ground thyme
and 1 teaspoon chopped mint
leaf

Vinaigrettes & Dressings

Another kitchen basic is the vinaigrette, best known as a topping for salads. Good cooks know, however, that many dressings can do double-duty, serving as a flavorful marinade for meats. They can even be used as dipping sauces for fruits and vegetables. The trick with vinaigrettes is to keep them blended—they're made of oil and vinegar, which separate very quickly. That's why it's best to prepare them as close to serving time as possible.

Basic Vinaigrette
Preparation time: 5 minutes
Yield: 8 tablespoons

2 tablespoons red wine vinegar
salt,to taste
1/8 teaspoon black pepper
3 tablespoons flax oil
3 tablespoons extra virgin olive oil

1. Place red wine vinegar, salt, and black pepper in small bowl and mix with wire whisk.
2. Add flax and olive oil, mix with wire whisk, and serve.

Nutrition Information Per Tablespoon

Calories 92	Fat 10 g	Fiber 0 g
Carbohydrates 0 g	Omega-3 Fats 3030 mg	Calcium 0 mg
Protein 0 g	Cholesterol 0 mg	Sodium 0 mg

Balsamic Vinaigrette

Preparation time: 5 minutes
Yield: 8 tablespoons

2 tablespoons balsamic vinegar
salt,to taste
1/8 teaspoon black pepper
3 tablespoons flax oil
3 tablespoons extra virgin olive oil

1. Place balsamic vinegar, salt, and pepper in bowl and mix with a wire whisk.
2. Add flax and olive oil, mix with wire whisk, and serve.

Nutrition Information Per Tablespoon

Calories 92	Fat 10 g	Fiber 0 g
Carbohydrates 0 g	Omega-3 Fats 3030 mg	Calcium 0 mg
Protein 0 g	Cholesterol 0 mg	Sodium 0 mg

Oriental Vinaigrette

Preparation time: 10 minutes
Yield: 9 tablespoons

1 tablespoon red wine vinegar
1 tablespoon white wine vinegar
1 teaspoon dried orange peel
1 teaspoon concentrated frozen orange juice (not diluted)
1 tablespoon fresh, finely chopped ginger root (or 1 teaspoon ground ginger)
salt, to taste
1/8 teaspoon black pepper
2 tablespoons flax oil
2 tablespoons canola oil
1 tablespoon sesame oil
2 tablespoons toasted flaxseed

1. Toast flaxseed and set aside to cool.
2. Place all ingredients in bowl, except oils and flaxseed, and mix.
3. Add oils slowly and mix with wire whip.
4. Add cooled toasted flaxseed and gently mix thoroughly, and serve.

Nutrition Information Per Tablespoon

Calories 84	Fat 9 g	Fiber 1 g
Carbohydrates 1 g	Omega-3 Fats 2650 mg	Calcium 7 mg
Protein 1 g	Cholesterol 0 mg	Sodium 0 mg

Roasted Tomato Vinaigrette
Preparation time: 60 minutes
Yield: 9 tablespoons

2 tablespoons balsamic vinegar
salt, to taste
1/8 teaspoon black pepper
1/4 cup roasted tomatoes
3 tablespoons flax oil
3 tablespoons extra virgin olive oil

1. Preheat oven at 350 F.
2. Slice 2 plum or Roma tomatoes 1/4 inch thick, lay on baking sheet, season with salt and pepper, and bake tomatoes approximately 60 minutes, or till dry.
3. Let tomatoes cool before chopping.
4. Mix vinegar and chopped tomato in small bowl.
5. Slowly add flax and olive oil, mix with wire whisk, and serve.

Nutrition Information Per Tablespoon

Calories 84	Fat 9 g	Fiber 0 g
Carbohydrates 1 g	Omega-3 Fats 2694 mg	Calcium 1 mg
Protein 0 g	Cholesterol 0 mg	Sodium 1 mg

Lemon Tarragon Vinaigrette
Preparation time: 5 minutes
Yield: 12 tablespoons

2 tablespoons white wine vinegar
1 tablespoon fresh lemon juice
salt, to taste
1/4 teaspoon black pepper
1 tablespoon Dijon mustard
1 tablespoon minced fresh tarragon or ½ tablespoon leaf tarragon
3 tablespoons flax oil
3 tablespoons extra virgin olive oil

1. Place all ingredients in small bowl, except oils, and mix with a wire whisk.
2. Add flax and olive oil, mix with wire whisk, and serve.

Nutrition Information Per Tablespoon

Calories 63	Fat 7 g	Fiber 0 g
Carbohydrates 0 g	Omega-3 Fats 2022 mg	Calcium 3 mg
Protein 0 g	Cholesterol 0 mg	Sodium 16 mg

Herb Vinaigrette
Preparation time: 5 minutes
Yield: 11 tablespoons

3 tablespoons balsamic vinegar
salt, to taste
1/2 tablespoon sugar
1/8 teaspoon black pepper
1 teaspoon fresh basil, chopped finely or leaf basil
1 teaspoon fresh parsley, chopped finely or parsley flakes
1 teaspoon oregano, chopped finely or ground oregano
3 tablespoons flax oil
3 tablespoons extra virgin olive oil

1. Place all ingredients in small bowl, except oils, and mix with a wire whisk.
2. Add flax and olive oil, mix with wire whisk, and serve.

Nutrition Information Per Tablespoon

Calories 70	Fat 8 g	Fiber 0 g
Carbohydrates 1 g	Omega-3 Fats 2210 mg	Calcium 3 mg
Protein 0 g	Cholesterol 0 mg	Sodium 0 mg

Mediterranean Vinaigrette
Preparation time: 5 minutes
Yield: 9 tablespoons

2 tablespoons balsamic vinegar
1 tablespoon fresh lemon juice
salt, to taste
1/2 tablespoon white sugar
1/8 teaspoon black pepper
2 tablespoons capers, chopped finely
1 tablespoon fresh parsley, chopped finely or 1 teaspoon parsley flakes
2 tablespoons flax oil
2 tablespoons extra virgin olive oil

1. Place all ingredients in small bowl, except oils, and mix with wire whisk.
2. Add flax and olive oil, mix with wire whisk, and serve.

Nutrition Information Per Tablespoon

Calories 58	Fat 6 g	Fiber 0 g
Carbohydrates 1 g	Omega-3 Fats 1799 mg	Calcium 2 mg
Protein 0 g	Cholesterol 0 mg	Sodium 57 mg

Cucumber Dill Dressing
Preparation time: 5 minutes
Yield: 12 tablespoons

1 tablespoon red wine vinegar
1 tablespoon white wine vinegar
1 tablespoon fresh lemon juice
2 teaspoons Dijon mustard
1 teaspoon honey
1 tablespoon fresh dill or 1 teaspoon dry
1/4 cup cucumber, diced, seedless, peeled
salt, to taste
1/8 teaspoon black pepper
3 tablespoons plain low-fat yogurt
2 tablespoons flax oil
2 tablespoons extra virgin olive oil

1. Place all ingredients in small bowl, except oils, and mix with a wire whisk.
2. Add flax oil and olive oil, mix with wire whisk, and serve.

Nutrition Information Per Tablespoon

Calories 47	Fat 5 g	Fiber 0 g
Carbohydrates 1 g	Omega-3 Fats 1347 mg	Calcium 10 mg
Protein 0 g	Cholesterol 0 mg	Sodium 14 mg

Honey Mustard Dressing
Preparation time: 5 minutes
Yield: 14 tablespoons

1 tablespoon red wine vinegar
1 tablespoon white wine vinegar
1 tablespoon fresh lemon juice
2 tablespoons Dijon mustard

2 tablespoons honey
salt, to taste
1/8 teaspoon black pepper
2 tablespoons plain low-fat yogurt
2 tablespoons flax oil
2 tablespoons extra virgin olive oil

1. Place all ingredients in small bowl, except oils, and mix with wire whisk.
2. Add oils, mix with wire whisk, and serve.

Nutrition Information Per Tablespoon

Calories 48	Fat 4 g	Fiber 0 g
Carbohydrates 3 g	Omega-3 Fats 1154 mg	Calcium 7 mg
Protein 0 g	Cholesterol 0 mg	Sodium 30 mg

Caesar Dressing
Preparation time: 5 minutes
Yield: 10 tablespoons

1 tablespoon red wine vinegar
1 tablespoon white wine vinegar
1 tablespoon fresh lemon juice
1 teaspoon Dijon mustard
salt, to taste
1/8 teaspoon black pepper
3 tablespoons plain low-fat yogurt
1/4 cup fresh shredded Parmesan cheese
2 tablespoons flax oil
2 tablespoons extra virgin olive oil

1. Place all ingredients in small bowl, except oils, and mix with wire whisk.
2. Add flax and olive oil, mix with wire whisk, and serve.

Nutrition Information Per Tablespoon

Calories 64	Fat 6 g	Fiber 0 g
Carbohydrates 1 g	Omega-3 Fats 1625 mg	Calcium 43 mg
Protein 1 g	Cholesterol 2 mg	Sodium 56 mg

Soups, Chili's and Chowders

4

What could be more enticing than a big bowl of soup? On a cold winter's day, the aroma of soup on the stove signifies comfort, warmth, and well-being, all by itself. For a formal dinner, soup is the traditional first course, setting the stage for the delights to come later in the meal. Whether served alone or in combination with other foods, soups—and their creamier relatives, chowders—are always welcome. And these days, making a rich, savory soup is easier than ever: although traditionalists are welcome to create their own soup stocks from scratch, there are plenty of no-fuss alternatives available, from canned broths to bouillon cubes. The choice is all yours!

Chili con Flax
Preparation time: 10 minutes
Cooking time: 25 minutes
Yield: 10 cups

Chili's a great warmer-upper, thanks to its savory seasonings, and that makes it a welcome choice for a light lunch in cooler weather. And real chili fans will tell you that it's a crowd-pleaser any time of the year. Our version uses turkey as its meat base. The toasted flax adds an extra piquancy to the sauce!

1 pound ground turkey
1 cup chopped onion
2 cloves garlic, minced
2 - 14.5 ounce cans stewed tomatoes (do not drain)
1 - 15 ounce can kidney beans, drained and rinsed
4 celery stalks, trimmed & chopped
1 tablespoon chili powder

salt, to taste
1 teaspoon Worcestershire sauce
1/2 teaspoon red pepper sauce or tabasco sauce (optional)
1/3 cup toasted flaxseed

1. In a stockpot, brown the turkey, onions, and garlic until the onions are transparent and the meat is lightly browned.
2. Add the stewed tomatoes to add moisture to the mix, followed by the kidney beans and chopped celery.
3. Stir and add the chili powder, salt, and Worcestershire sauce.
4. If you or your family like their chili on the spicy side, use red pepper sauce or tabasco for that extra "kick." For those who like it mild, you can leave them out. If the chili appears to be a bit thick, add a small amount of water to suite your tastes! In either case, simmer about 5-10 minutes uncovered.
5. Spoon out into individual serving bowls and top with a sprinkling of toasted flax seed.

Nutrition Information Per Cup

Calories 181	Fat 7 g	Fiber 6g
Carbohydrates 18 g	Omega-3 Fats 1536 mg	Calcium 77 mg
Protein 14 g	Cholesterol 36 mg	Sodium 299 mg

Chicken Noodle Soup
Preparation time: 15 minutes
Cooking time: 10 minutes
Yield: 8 cups

For many of us, chicken soup is the ultimate comfort food. Served before the entree at dinner or as a companion course with a sandwich at lunch, there's nothing better! And what a great way to use the leftovers from last night's roast chicken!

6 cups reduced sodium chicken broth
1 cup cooked chicken meat, cubed
1 stalk celery, trimmed, diced

1/4 cup onion, diced
1 cup Hodgson Mill flax noodles(penne or spiral), uncooked or
homemade pasta (recipe, page 83)
black pepper, to taste
fresh chopped parsley, to garnish
¼ cup toasted flaxseed

1. In a stockpot, combine broth, chicken, celery, and onion. Bring to a full rolling boil.
2. Add flax noodles. Cook uncovered until tender, about 9 or 10 minutes after water returns to a boil.
3. In the final few minutes of cooking, add black pepper as desired.
4. Ladle out into individual bowls, garnished with a sprinkling of chopped parsley and toasted flaxseed.

Nutrition Information Per Cup

Calories 95	Fat 3 g	Fiber 3g
Carbohydrates 6 g	Omega-3 Fats 1412 mg	Calcium 19 mg
Protein 10 g	Cholesterol 15 mg	Sodium 485 mg

New England Clam Chowder
Preparation time: 30 minutes
Cooking time: 30 minutes
Yield: 9 cups

Rich, creamy New England Clam Chowder can be a meal all on its own. In our recipe, we use the distinctive flavor of flax to add a mildly nutty zest to this traditional dish.

2 slices raw bacon, diced
1 medium onion, diced
1 stalk celery, trimmed, diced
2 medium potatoes, with skins, cut into 1/3" - ½" pieces
2 cloves fresh garlic, minced or ½ teaspoon granulated garlic
1/4 cup ground flaxseed (golden flaxseed blends best)
2 cups reduced sodium chicken broth

2 cups skim milk
salt, to taste
2 - 6.5 ounce can clams, with juice, do not drain juice
1/2 teaspoon fresh thyme or ground thyme
white pepper, to taste
Chopped parsley, for garnish

1. In the bottom of a pre-heated stockpot, using medium heat, brown the bacon until the pieces are crisp. Do not drain.
2. Add the diced onion and celery and cook at medium heat until they become transparent.
3. Add potatoes, cooking to medium-low heat, until they are warm in the center. Stir frequently while cooking to avoid browning.
4. Add garlic to the mixture, cooking for approximately 30 seconds.
5. Mix in ground flaxseed, making sure that it coats all ingredients, and cook for approximately 1 more minute.
6. Add chicken broth, stirring well. Add milk and salt, simmer for 10 minutes covered. For the next 10 minutes, cook uncovered.
7. When 20 minutes are up, add the clams, clam juice, and thyme. Add pepper to taste. Spoon into individual serving bowls, with a garnish of chopped parsley.

Nutrition Information Per Cup

Calories 85	Fat 2 g	Fiber 2 g
Carbohydrates 13 g	Omega-3 Fats 866 mg	Calcium 94 mg
Protein 5 g	Cholesterol 3 mg	Sodium 277 mg

Corn Chowder
Preparation time: 10 minutes
Cooking time: 35 minutes
Yield: 7 cups

This chowder is another traditional favorite, and a great veggie alternative to the fish-based chowders. We think you'll find that the addition of flax provides a smooth, complementary flavor to this dish.

1 tablespoon extra virgin olive oil
1 medium onion, diced
1 stalk celery, trimmed, diced
2 potatoes, with skins, diced
2 cloves garlic, minced
1 – 15 ounce can corn, whole kernel(drained)
2 cups reduced sodium chicken broth
3 cups skim milk
salt, to taste
3 tablespoons ground flaxseed
black pepper, to taste
Fresh chopped parsley, for garnish

1. Preheat your stockpot over medium heat, then add the olive oil, being careful not to spatter.
2. Add the diced onion and celery and cook until the pieces become transparent.
3. Add potatoes and continue cooking until they are warm in the center. Stir frequently to avoid browning.
4. Next add the garlic and the corn, cooking for approximately 30 seconds.
5. Add chicken broth to the pot, stirring well. Reduce heat to simmer, then add milk and salt. Cook covered for approximately 30 minutes.
6. Add pepper to taste and ground flax. Cook for another 5 minutes, or until slightly thickened to a velvety texture.
7. Spoon into individual serving bowls, each topped with a sprinkling of parsley.

Nutrition Information Per Cup

Calories 177	Fat 4 g	Fiber 4 g
Carbohydrates 29 g	Omega-3 Fats 844 mg	Calcium 155 mg
Protein 8 g	Cholesterol 2 mg	Sodium 359 mg

Butternut Squash Soup
Preparation time: 5 minutes
Cooking time: 1 hour 30 minutes
Yield: 6 cups

This great standby is a traditional autumn dish. It makes a wonderful first course for Thanksgiving dinner, but your family will welcome a bowl of it any time. For the convenience of busy households, you'll find that you can prepare the squash (step 2) the night before, to save on production time!

1 butternut squash
2 tablespoons unsalted butter
1 leek, white portion only, chopped
1 tablespoon fresh ground ginger or ½ teaspoon ground ginger
6 cups reduced sodium vegetable or chicken broth
salt and pepper to taste
chopped cilantro, for garnish
1/4 cup toasted flaxseed

1. Preheat oven to 400 F.
2. Prepare a baking sheet by coating it lightly with a nonstick spray. Cut squash in half and scoop out the seeds. Then place the squash on the pan, cut sides down. Bake in oven about 1 hour, until the squash is tender. Remove from oven, scoop pulp into a medium mixing bowl, and discard the skin. Set bowl aside.
3. Over medium heat, melt butter in a stockpot. Add the chopped leek and ginger and cook over medium heat about 5 to 8 minutes, until the leek is tender.
4. Stir in the cooked squash, along with 4 cups of broth. Simmer over low heat covered for about 20 minutes, then remove from heat.
5. Puree the squash mixture in your blender or food processor until smooth, making sure pressure does not build up in the blender from the heat.
6. Return the puree mixture to the stockpot and add the remaining broth, stirring to keep the mixture consistent. Simmer for about 5 more minutes, adding salt and pepper to taste.

7. Spoon into soup bowls, dust the tops with toasted flaxseed and a sprinkling of cilantro, if desired.

Nutrition Information Per Cup

Calories 106	Fat 4 g	Fiber 3 g
Carbohydrates 14 g	Omega-3 Fats 1823 mg	Calcium 69 mg
Protein 6 g	Cholesterol 2 mg	Sodium 577 mg

Chicken-Dumpling Soup
Preparation time: 30 minutes
Cooking time: 20 minutes
Yield: 6 cups

Here's another soup with a down-home flair. And it's a big favorite with kids, who find the fluffy dumplings irresistible!

Soup Base
6 cups reduced sodium chicken broth
1 cup cooked chicken meat, cubed
1 stalk celery, trimmed, diced
1/4 cup onion, diced
black pepper, to taste
Fresh chopped parsley, for garnish

Dumplings
1/4 cup all purpose flour
1/4 cup whole wheat flour
1-1/2 tablespoons unsalted butter
1 teaspoon baking powder
1/4 cup ground flaxseed
1/3 cup skim milk

1. In a large stockpot, combine the broth, chicken, celery, and onions. Over medium heat, bring to a boil.

2. Add pepper to taste, then reduce to a simmer uncovered while you prepare your dumpling mix.

3. Place flours in a medium-sized mixing bowl. Cut the butter into the flours until it forms walnut-sized pieces.

4. Add remaining dry ingredients, stirring to make sure they blend completely.

5. Add milk gradually, mixing as you go until a thick batter is formed.

6. Bring soup back up to full boil.

7. Using a medium-sized wooden spoon or cookie scoop, drop about a tablespoon of dumpling mixture, one at a time, onto the surface.

8. Keep the soup boiling and cook uncovered for 10 minutes, then cover and cook for another 10 minutes. When the dumplings are not doughy, then it is done.

9. Spoon soup into individual serving bowls, making sure that each gets two to three dumpling. Garnish with a sprinkling of parsley.

Nutrition Information Per Cup

Calories 148	Fat 6 g	Fiber 3 g
Carbohydrates 10 g	Omega-3 Fats 1332 mg	Calcium 85 mg
Protein 13 g	Cholesterol 28 mg	Sodium 738 mg

Penne Tomato Soup
Preparation time: 10 minutes
Cooking time: 45 minutes
Yield: 8 cups

Add an Italian flair to your soup repertoire with this delicious soup. It goes great with a crisp mixed green salad.

1 cup Hodgson Mill flax penne noodles, uncooked or
homemade pasta (recipe, page 83)
1 tablespoon unsalted butter or extra virgin olive oil
1 medium onion, minced
2- 14.5 ounces can Italian plum tomatoes, diced

1-14 ounce can vegetable broth
1/3 cup evaporated skim milk
salt and pepper, to taste
1/3 cup Parmesan cheese, grated

1. Cook pasta according to directions, drain, and set aside.
2. In a 3 quart saucepan, melt butter over low heat or heat olive oil, then add onions and cook about five minutes, until the pieces are translucent.
3. Add tomatoes and vegetable broth, then bring the liquid to simmer and cook for 10 minutes covered.
4. Add evaporated skim milk, stirring constantly, then continue simmering for another 5 minutes.
5. Add salt and pepper to taste, then spoon the pasta into the soup mixture.
6. Simmer another minute or so, just long enough to reheat the pasta.
7. Spoon into serving bowls, and top each with a sprinkling of grated Parmesan cheese.

Nutrition Information Per Cup

Calories 94	Fat 4 g	Fiber 2 g
Carbohydrates 12 g	Omega-3 Fats 108 mg	Calcium 94 mg
Protein 4 g	Cholesterol 4 mg	Sodium 335 mg

Portabello Flax Soup

Preparation time: 15 minutes
Cooking time: 20 minutes
Yield: 7 cups

The rich, meaty taste of portabello mushrooms are well-complemented by the nutty taste of ground flax. This makes a great soup to start an elegant dinner, but it's a wonderful choice anytime you want to feel just a little pampered.

1 - 2 tablespoons unsalted butter
1 pound portabello mushrooms, finely chopped

3 cloves garlic, finely chopped
2 tablespoons light or dark miso(bean paste)
4 cups vegetable broth
2 cups skim milk
3 tablespoons ground flaxseed
1/4 teaspoon ground cumin
1/4 teaspoon ground thyme
1/4 teaspoon leaf rosemary
salt and pepper, to taste

1. Preheat your stockpot, over low heat, then add butter.
2. When the butter melts, add the chopped mushrooms and cook over gentle heat for 2 minutes.
3. Add the garlic, then saute the mixture for 1 minute. Add miso and stir thoroughly.
4. Add vegetable broth and milk, then simmer covered for about 10 minutes, stirring occasionally.
5. Add the ground flax, cumin, thyme, and rosemary and simmer another 5 minutes, then taste and, if desired, add a pinch of salt and pepper.
6. Spoon out into individual serving bowls, or present in a serving tureen and allow friends or family to serve themselves.

Nutrition Information Per Cup

Calories 92	Fat 4 g	Fiber 2 g
Carbohydrates 10 g	Omega-3 Fats 861 mg	Calcium 108 mg
Protein 5 g	Cholesterol 6 mg	Sodium 763 mg

Curry Pumpkin Soup
Preparation time: 10 minutes
Cooking time: 20 minutes
Yield: 4 cups

Here's another classic autumn dish. It's a wonderful supper selection, just right to warm your kids' tummies before they head out to make their Halloween rounds in the neighborhood. And the aroma while cooking! Delicious!

1 -15 ounce can 100% pure solid pumpkin
2 cups skim milk
3 cloves garlic, minced
1 tablespoon fresh ginger, grated
2 teaspoons curry powder
2 tablespoons ground flaxseed
1 cup apple juice
salt and pepper to taste
fresh cilantro, chopped, for garnish
2 tablespoons toasted flaxseed

1. In a large stockpot, combine pumpkin and milk, mixing well.
2. Cook over medium heat for about 5 minutes, then add garlic and ginger and continue cooking another 5 minutes.
3. Stir in curry powder and ground flaxseed, then add the apple juice to moisten the mixture.
4. Bring to a simmer (be careful not to let it come to a boil) covered, then remove from heat. If desired, add salt and pepper to taste.
5. Spoon into individual serving bowls, top with toasted flaxseed and cilantro.

Nutrition Information Per Cup

Calories 162	Fat 5 g	Fiber 6 g
Carbohydrates 24 g	Omega-3 Fats 2274 mg	Calcium 216 mg
Protein 8 g	Cholesterol 2 mg	Sodium 74 mg

Bean Soup
Preparation time: 10 minutes
Cooking time: 30 minutes
Yield: 5 cups

This wonderful soup is rich in fiber, and will keep you full for several hours!!

1 tablespoon extra virgin olive oil
1 medium onion, coarsely chopped
1 medium carrot, peeled and diced
1 celery stalk, trimmed, diced
3 cloves garlic, chopped finely
3 cups vegetable broth
1/4 cup ground flaxseed
1 -15 ounce can cooked beans (Navy or Great Northern), washed and drained
salt and pepper, to taste
Fresh chopped parsley, for garnish

1. Preheat your stockpot, then add oil, onion, carrot, and celery. Over medium heat, saute these vegetables for 5 to 8 minutes, until the pieces are lightly browned.
2. Add the garlic, and continue to saute for another minute.
3. Add ground flaxseed and the vegetable broth, then simmer the whole mixture covered for about 15 minutes, being careful to keep the pot from reaching a boil.
4. Add beans, salt and pepper(to taste),and continue cooking for about 5 minutes more.
5. Ladle into serving bowls and garnish with fresh parsley. Accompany each bowl with a slice of whole grain bread for a satisfyingly filling meal.

Nutrition Information Per Cup

Calories 176	Fat 6 g	Fiber 8 g
Carbohydrates 23 g	Omega-3 Fats 1633 mg	Calcium 85 mg
Protein 9 g	Cholesterol 0 mg	Sodium 589 mg

Julie's Cream of Mushroom Soup
Preparation time: 10 minutes
Cooking time: 20 minutes

Yield: 5 cups

Julie Kamenetzky of Pittsburg, Pennsylvania offers this savory treat. She started experimenting in cooking with flax when her father-in-law began experiencing heart problems, and she found herself looking for more heart-healthy alternatives to cooking for her family. This is just one of the family favorites she's come up with.

8 ounces fresh mushrooms, with stems
1-2 teaspoons unsalted butter
2 cups reduced sodium chicken broth
1 stalk celery, trimmed, diced
1/4 cup onions, chopped
1/8 cup fresh parsley, minced
salt and pepper, to taste

Cream sauce
1-2 teaspoons unsalted butter
2 tablespoons ground flax
1 cup skim milk

1. In a large saucepan or stock pot, saute mushrooms in butter for a few minutes.
2. Add chicken broth, celery, onions, and parsley. Simmer, covered for about 15 minutes.
3. While the vegetables are cooking, make the cream sauce by melting butter in medium saucepan over low heat.
4. Slowly add ground flaxseed and blend in well, about 1 minute.
5. Stir milk in slowly with a wire whisk and cook until thickened and smooth, about 5 minutes.
6. After the vegetables are cooked, drain, reserving the stock.
7. Blend vegetables in a food processor.
8. Pour the cream sauce slowly into the stock, cook and stir until the soup has just reaches a boil.

9. Add the ground vegetables. Add salt and pepper to taste.

Nutrition Information Per Cup

Calories 75	Fat 4 g	Fiber 2 g
Carbohydrates 6 g	Omega-3 Fats 797 mg	Calcium 78 mg
Protein 5 g	Cholesterol 8 mg	Sodium 265 mg

A Taste of Italy

5

Flax is a natural for pasta dishes, whether it's incorporated into your pasta dough or included in your sauces. For a double dose of the great benefits of this wonderful seed, try doing both. Great ready-made flax-based pastas are available on the market, but those of you who like to cook from scratch might want to try your hand at the recipe we've included here.

Homemade Pasta Dough
Preparation time: 40 minutes
Cooking time: 5-8 minutes
Yield: 8 servings

1 ½ cups all-purpose flour
1/2 cup ground flaxseed
2 large eggs
2 tablespoons extra virgin oil

1. Mix flax and flour in large bowl.
2. In medium bowl, beat eggs, add oil, and mix thoroughly.
3. On table, sprinkle flour and place flour/flax mixture on table. You may keep mixture in bowl, if you prefer. Shape flour/flax mixture in the shape of a well, add egg/oil mixture inside of well.
4. Slowly mix starting inside of well and working out. Knead dough for about 5 minutes.
5. Wrap with plastic and leave sit on counter for 30 minutes.
6. Roll into desired shape and cook.

Nutrition Information Per Serving

Calories 170	Fat 8 g	Fiber 3 g
Carbohydrates 18 g	Omega-3 Fats 1964 mg	Calcium 84 mg
Protein 6 g	Cholesterol 53 mg	Sodium 19 mg

Classic Pasta Sauces

All great pasta dishes need great sauces. From classic carbonara to piquant pesto, here are the traditional standards of Italian cuisine. Not all the sauces below include flax, like the marinara recipe below. In those cases, just make sure to serve the sauce atop flax-based pasta!

Uncle David's Marinara Sauce
Preparation time: 5 minutes
Cooking time: 25 minutes
Yield: 5 cups

My Uncle Dave came up with this variation on the traditional marinara sauce because he wanted a healthier alternative to the high-sodium, store-bought varieties. You can make it up in a large batch and freeze it so you'll always have some on hand when your family is clamoring for a spaghetti supper! This is a main component of many other recipes and will be referred to often!

1 tablespoon extra virgin olive oil
4 cloves garlic, minced
1 - 28 ounce can crushed tomatoes
1 - 14.5 ounce can diced tomatoes
1/2 teaspoon crushed red pepper flakes
2 tablespoons fresh chopped parley or parsley flakes
1/2 teaspoon dried oregano
Salt and pepper to taste

1. In a 2-quart saucepan, heat the olive oil until fragrant. Add garlic and cook on medium heat until soft.

2. Stir in both types of tomatoes and reduce heat to simmer covered for 20 minutes. Add red pepper, parsley, and oregano and simmer for about 5 more minutes. Stir occasionally, adjusting seasonings to taste.

Nutrition Information Per Cup

Calories 96	Fat 3 g	Fiber 3 g
Carbohydrates 17 g	Omega-3 Fats 29 mg	Calcium 88 mg
Protein 3 g	Cholesterol 0 mg	Sodium 528 mg

Alfredo Sauce
Preperation time: 5 minutes
Cooking time: 15 minutes
Yield: 4 cups

The creamy flavors of a good alfredo sauce provides a fine vehicle for the nutty taste of flax. Just remember to hold off adding flaxseed in this and any other sauces until the end, to avoid unpleasant textures caused by over-cooking.

1/3 stick unsalted butter
1/8 cup all-purpose flour
2 cups skim milk
1 – 14 ounce can reduced sodium chicken broth
1/4 teaspoon granulated garlic
salt and pepper, to taste
1/2 cup Parmesan cheese, grated
½ cup ground flaxseed (prefer golden)

1. Melt butter in saucepan. Add flour and mix making a roux.
2. Slowly add milk and blend well and cook low-medium heat .
3. Add chicken broth, garlic, and salt and pepper to taste.
4. When starting to thicken, add Parmesan cheese. When almost thickened, take off heat.
5. Mix in flaxseed with wire whisk, let set until fully thickened, and garnish with parsley.

Nutrition Information Per 1/2 Cup

Calories 131	Fat 9 g	Fiber 3 g
Carbohydrates 5 g	Omega-3 Fats 2008 mg	Calcium 182 mg
Protein 7 g	Cholesterol 16 mg	Sodium 298 mg

Pesto

Preparation time: 5 minutes
Yield: 8 tablespoons

1 tablespoon extra virgin olive oil
1 tablespoon shredded Parmesan cheese
4 tablespoons ground flaxseed
1 clove garlic
1 tablespoon pine nuts
1/4 cup fresh basil

1. Place all ingredients except basil in blender, food processor, or small chopper/grinder.
2. Pureed until paste is formed. Make sure you add basil last, or after you have made a paste to prevent discoloration or darkening of the basil.

Nutrition Information Per Tablespoon

Calories 37	Fat 4 g	Fiber 1 g
Carbohydrates 0 g	Omega-3 Fats 968 mg	Calcium 20 mg
Protein 1 g	Cholesterol 0 mg	Sodium 12 mg

Carbonara

Preparation time: 5 minutes
Cooking time: 15 minutes
Yield: 3 Cups

This delicate, cheesy sauce needs to be used as soon as possible after it's prepared, if you want to enjoy it at it's best!

1/3 cup ground flaxseed
2 cups skim milk
1 cup reduced sodium chicken broth
1/4 teaspoon garlic powder
½ cup fresh shredded Parmesan cheese
pepper and salt, to taste
1 tablespoon unsalted butter

1. In a 3 quart saucepan, whisk flax into cold milk and broth, and heat over low-medium heat.
2. Constantly stir with wire whisk until sauce thickens.
3. Take off heat and add garlic, parmesan cheese, and salt and pepper to taste.
4. Fold in butter until smooth and creamy. Remove from heat.

Nutrition Information Per 1/2 Cup

Calories 116	Fat 7 g	Fiber 2 g
Carbohydrates 5 g	Omega-3 Fats 1642 mg	Calcium 232 mg
Protein 8 g	Cholesterol 13 mg	Sodium 295 mg

Now that you've mastered the traditional repertoire of a good Italian kitchen, let's see how we can put these tasty sauces to work in some tasty entrees that will have your family asking for more! And, of course, we'll be featuring flax-based pasta, right?

Fettuccine Carbonara
Preparation time: 15 minutes
Cooking time: 30 minutes
Yield: 4 servings

8 ounces Hodgson Mill fettuccine flax noodles, dry
or homemade pasta (recipe, page 83)
4 strips bacon, cooked, chopped
1 cup frozen peas
Carbonara sauce

1. Cook noodles according to directions. Drain and place noodles in large bowl.
2. Mix bacon and peas into hot noodles.
3. Mix cream sauce into noodle mixture.

Nutrition Information Per Serving

Calories 428	Fat 14 g	Fiber 12 g
Carbohydrates 52 g	Omega-3 Fats 3143 mg	Calcium 356 mg
Protein 24 g	Cholesterol 24 mg	Sodium 591 mg

Spaghetti w/ Turkey Meatballs
Preparation time: 20 minutes
Cooking time: 40 minutes
Yield: 8 servings

Everybody loves this classic of Italian cuisine, from the seasoned gastronome to the finickiest child. What makes our version truly special are the meatballs, fortified with the great taste of flax.

8 ounces Hodgson Mill flax spaghetti noodles
or homemade pasta (recipe, page 83)
noodles, cooked and drained
Uncle David's Marinara Sauce (recipe, page 84)

Meatballs

8 ounces lean ground beef (round or sirloin)
8 ounces ground turkey
1/4 cup ground flaxseed
2 egg whites
3 tablespoons red wine(optional)
2 tablespoons tomato paste
salt, to taste
1/8 teaspoon black pepper
1/4 cup onion, chopped finely
1 clove garlic, chopped finely
1/2 cup shredded Parmesan cheese
1/4 cup bread crumbs
seasoned flour
2 tablespoons extra virgin olive oil

1. Mix all ingredients, except seasoned flour and oil, in large bowl together. Shape into balls. A one-inch diameter works well, but every cook has his or her own personal preference.
2. Dredge the formed balls in seasoned flour; brown in large skillet with olive oil until interior of the balls are fully cooked. Turn frequently to make certain that all sides are brown.
3. Drain pan, add marinara sauce and simmer for 10 minutes.
4. Serve over hot pasta.

Nutrition Information Per Serving

Calories 339	Fat 13 g	Fiber 7 g
Carbohydrates 35 g	Omega-3 Fats 1408 mg	Calcium 144 mg
Protein 21 g	Cholesterol 44 mg	Sodium 531 mg

Baked Tube Lasagna
Preparation time: 15 minutes
Cooking time: 45 minutes
Yield: 8 servings

This popular dish is always welcome at our table. In this version, the flax is built right into the pasta and there's even more in the sausage. To up the flax content even further, try setting out a bowl of toasted flaxseed alongside the grated parmesan. It makes a tasty sprinkle-on topping. By the way, you'll find the sausage recipe very versatile—it appears in a number of the recipes that follow!

1 – 12 ounce box Hodgson Mill flax Penne noodles,
or homemade pasta (recipe, page 83)
1 cup part-skim ricotta cheese
1 egg
1/4 cup Parmesan cheese, shredded
salt and pepper, to taste
4 ounces part-skim mozzarella cheese, shredded
1 pound Flax Italian Sausage
Uncle David's Marinara Sauce (recipe, page 84)

Lasagna recipe

1. Preheat oven to 325 F.
2. Cook pasta according to directions, and set aside.
3. In small bowl, mix ricotta cheese, egg, and parmesan together. Season with salt and pepper. Set aside.
4. Spray 9 X 13 pan with non-stick cooking spray.

Assembling the lasagna

Pour 1/3 of the marinara sauce into the bottom of the baking pan, spreading evenly. On top of this sauce, make a layer of the cooked pasta, using 1/2 of the total amount prepared. Top the pasta with the entire volume of cheese mixture, spreading it to the edges to form a smooth layer. Next add the sausage, again spreading it evenly. Pour half of the remaining marinara sauce over all, then create a final layer of pasta. Pour the last of the marinara on top, then add the Mozzarella. Bake covered for 45 minutes.

Nutrition Information Per Serving

Calories 446	Fat 18 g	Fiber 10 g
Carbohydrates 45 g	Omega-3 Fats 2572 mg	Calcium 300 mg
Protein 28 g	Cholesterol 91 mg	Sodium 542 mg

Flax Italian Sausage

Preparation time: 5 minutes
Cooking time: 15 minutes
Yield: 1 pound

1 teaspoon granulated garlic
2 teaspoons Italian seasoning
2 teaspoons parsley flakes
1 teaspoon black pepper
1 teaspoon fennel seeds
½ teaspoon leaf oregano
salt, to taste
½ teaspoon red pepper flakes
1 pound ground turkey
1/2 cup onion, minced
1/2 cup ground flaxseed

1. Mix spices together first in small bowl.
2. Cook meat with onion in skillet until done, then add spices.
3. When cooked together well, take off heat, and add flaxseed.

Nutrition Information Per 3 Ounce Serving

Calories 171	Fat 11 g	Fiber 4 g
Carbohydrates 2 g	Omega-3 Fats 2363 mg	Calcium 48 mg
Protein 16 g	Cholesterol 60 mg	Sodium 76 mg

Vegetable Lasagna
Preparation time: 20 minutes
Cooking time: 60-65 minutes
Yield: 8 servings

The wonderful thing about pasta is that it lends itself so well to vegetarian cooking. Even committed carnivores have been known to request this tasty variation on the lasagna theme.

1 – 12 ounce box Hodgson Mill flax fettuccine noodles,
or homemade pasta (recipe, page 83)
1 small eggplant, cut into ½ inch slices
1 zucchini, cut into ½ inch slices
1 Portabello mushroom, cut into ½ inch slices, stem removed
1 tablespoon extra virgin olive oil
2 cups part-skim ricotta cheese
2 eggs
1/4 cup Parmesan cheese, shredded
salt and pepper, to taste
4 ounces part-skim mozzarella cheese, shredded
Uncle David's Marinara Sauce (recipe, page 84)

1. Preheat oven to 400 F.
2. Cook pasta according to directions, and set aside.
3. In a bowl, toss eggplant, zucchini, and portabella mushrooms together in the olive oil.
4. Spread all ingredients evenly on a baking sheet. Roast in oven for 20 minutes, turning at least once to avoid over-browning. Remove from oven and set aside. Reduce oven heat to 350 F.
5. In small bowl, mix ricotta cheese, eggs, and Parmesan cheese together. Season with salt and pepper. Set aside.
6. Spray 9 X 13 pan with non-stick cooking spray.

Assembling the lasagna

Pour 1/3 of the marinara sauce into the bottom of the baking pan, spreading evenly. On top of this sauce, make a layer of the cooked pasta, using ½ of the total amount prepared. Top the pasta with ½ of the cheese mixture, spreading it to the edges to form a smooth layer. Next add ½ of the vegetables, spreading evenly. Pour another 1/3 of the marinara sauce. Next, top with the rest of the pasta. Then add the rest of the cheese mixture. Then, put rest of the vegetables. End with the rest of the marinara sauce. Top with mozzarella cheese. Bake covered at 350 F. for 40-45 minutes.

Nutrition Information Per Serving

Calories 403	Fat 14 g	Fiber 9 g
Carbohydrates 49 g	Omega-3 Fats 627 mg	Calcium 359 mg
Protein 21 g	Cholesterol 82 mg	Sodium 534 mg

Stuffed Shells
Preparation time: 15 minutes
Cooking time: 40 minutes
Yield: 4 servings

These stuffed shells are easy to make, especially if you took our advice earlier and made up the marinara sauce in advance!

12 large pasta shells
Flax Italian Sausage(1/2 recipe)
1 ½ cups Uncle David's Marinara Sauce (recipe, page 84)

Cheese mixture
1 cup part-skim ricotta cheese
2 tablespoons grated Parmesan cheese
1 whole egg, raw
salt and pepper to taste

1. Preheat oven to 350 F.

2. Cook pasta shells according to package directions. Rinse and set aside.

3. In a bowl, blend cheese mixture together until smooth.

4. Coat the bottom and sides of a 9 X 9 pan with non-stick spray, then pour 1 cup Uncle David's Marinara sauce on bottom of pan, using spoon to spread evenly.

5. Fill shells 1/2 full with Italian sausage mixture, and then top with ricotta cheese mixture.

6. Place shells on top of marinara sauce and pour remaining sauce on shells.

7. Bake covered in 350 F. oven for 30 minutes, serve garnished with fresh shredded Parmesan cheese.

Nutrition Information Per Serving

Calories 386	Fat 17 g	Fiber 5 g
Carbohydrates 34 g	Omega-3 Fats 2067 mg	Calcium 273 mg
Protein 26 g	Cholesterol 119 mg	Sodium 384 mg

Marinara Chicken
Preparation time: 10 minutes
Cooking time: 20 minutes
Yield: 4 servings

The noodles and the breading are the key for this dish—both are flax based. You'll find, as we did, that the taste of flax works very well with chicken!

12 ounces Hodgson Mill Flax Fettuccini Noodles or
Homemade pasta (recipe, page 83)
Uncle David's Marinara Sauce (recipe, page 84)
4 boneless, skinless chicken breasts (4 ounces each)
seasoned flour (recipe, page 56)
egg wash (recipe, page 56)
Basic flax breading (recipe, page 57)
1-2 tablespoons extra virgin olive oil
2 tablespoons shredded Parmesan Cheese

freshly chopped parsley or parsley flakes, to garnish

1. Cook pasta according to directions, rinse, and set aside.
2. Heat marinara sauce over low-medium heat.
3. While marinara sauce is cooking, dredge chicken breast with seasoned flour, then egg wash, and then coat with basic breading mix.
4. Place olive oil in large saucepan, add chicken breasts, and cook until golden brown, approximately 4 minutes on each side.
5. Place pasta in 4 bowls, equally distribute marinara sauce, top with cooked chicken breast, garnish with shredded Parmesan cheese and chopped parsley.

Nutrition Information Per Serving

Calories 594	Fat 19 g	Fiber 13 g
Carbohydrates 67 g	Omega-3 Fats 2736 mg	Calcium 200 mg
Protein 41 g	Cholesterol 68 mg	Sodium 849 mg

Baked Mostaccioli
Preparation time: 20 minutes
Cooking time: 25 minutes
Yield: 6 servings

The Monterey Jack cheese in this dish adds just the right touch of sharpness! And, of course, it goes best over flax-based pasta.

8 ounces Hodgson Mill Flax Penne Noodles, dry, or
homemade pasta (recipe, page 83)
3 cups Uncle David's Marinara Sauce (recipe, page 84)
1/4 cup fresh shredded Parmesan cheese
1/2 cup Monterey Jack cheese, shredded

1. Preheat oven to 350 F.
2. Cook pasta according to directions.
3. Heat marinara sauce until bubbly and hot.

4. Mix cooked pasta noodles with marinara sauce.

5. Prepare an 8x8 pan with non-stick spray on bottom and sides. Put pasta and sauce mixture into pan, top with cheeses, and bake covered in 350 F oven for 25-30 minutes.

Nutrition Information Per Serving

Calories 230	Fat 6 g	Fiber 6 g
Carbohydrates 35 g	Omega-3 Fats 468 mg	Calcium 147 mg
Protein 10 g	Cholesterol 9 mg	Sodium 371 mg

Gourmet Mushrooms and Artichokes over Spiral Pasta
Preparation time: 10 minutes
Cooking time: 12 minutes
Yield: 6 (8 oz) Servings

Pasta dishes are wonderfully versatile. They can be plain and simple, or they can add a touch of elegance to any table. This dish will delight even the most sophisticated palate, and even vegetarians can enjoy it without guilt! By the way, we like the combination of portabello, crimini, and shiitake mushrooms, but feel free to experiment with other types if you wish.

1 – 10 ounce box Hodgson Mill Flax Spiral Noodles
or homemade pasta (recipe, page 83)
1 tablespoon unsalted butter
2 tablespoons extra virgin olive oil
1 tablespoon chopped finely shallots
1 cup sliced Portabello mushrooms
1/2 cup sliced crimini mushrooms
1/2 cup sliced shiitake mushrooms
2 tablespoons white wine (optional)
2 tablespoons all-purpose flour
1 cup skim milk
1 – 13.75 ounce can quartered artichokes, drained
1/2 cup diced canned tomatoes
Salt and pepper to taste

Fresh, chopped parsley for garnish

1. Cook pasta according to directions. Drain and place in large bowl.
2. Place butter and olive oil in saucepan. Over medium heat, add shallots and cook and stir.
3. Add all mushrooms, continuing to cook and stir over medium heat, about 5 minutes.
4. Add the wine.
5. Add 1/2 cup milk and all the flour, and blend in well.
6. Add the remaining milk and cook until slightly thickened, approximately 1 minute.
7. Toss with hot cooked pasta.
8. Add the artichokes and tomato.
9. Garnish with fresh parsley and serve hot.

Nutrition Information Per Serving

Calories 333	Fat 8 g	Fiber 9 g
Carbohydrates 55 g	Omega-3 Fats 615 mg	Calcium 80 mg
Protein 12 g	Cholesterol 6 mg	Sodium 76 mg

Linguini with Shrimp Sauce
Preparation time: 20 minutes
Cooking time: 5 minutes
Yield: 4 servings

Here's another sophisticated dish to tempt your palate. The secret to success is to avoid overcooking the shrimp!

8 ounces Hodgson Mill Flax Spaghetti or Fettuccine noodles, or homemade pasta (recipe, page 83)
1 tablespoon extra virgin olive oil
1/4 cup chopped shallots
1/4 teaspoon chopped garlic
8 ounces shrimp, peeled, deveined, raw
1/4 cup fresh basil leaf, cut into thin strips

2 Roma tomatoes, peeled, seeded, chopped
4 tablespoons Marsala wine(optional)
Salt and pepper to taste

1. Cook pasta according to directions.
2. In a large saucepan, sauté the shallots and garlic in olive oil. Add the shrimp and cook for about 3 min. Then add the tomatoes, basil leaf, and wine, adjust seasoning. Serve over hot pasta.
3. At the table, make sure you set out bowls of freshly grated parmesan cheese for your diners to spoon on their servings, if they so choose.

Nutrition Information Per Serving

Calories 324	Fat 7 g	Fiber 8 g
Carbohydrates 46 g	Omega-3 Fats 1007 mg	Calcium 41 mg
Protein 20 g	Cholesterol 86 mg	Sodium 91 mg

Penne with Four Cheeses
Preparation time: 10 minutes
Cooking time: 15 minutes
Yield: 6 servings

The combination of cheeses makes this a truly distinctive choice. Take care to keep stirring when you're melting the cheese—you want a smooth, velvety sauce with no scorching.

1 pound Hodgson Mill Flax Penne Noodles,
or homemade pasta (recipe, page 83)
1 tablespoon unsalted butter
2 ounces fontina cheese
2 ounces gorgonzola cheese
2 ounces boursin cheese
1/2 cup freshly shredded parmesan cheese
1 cup skim milk
1/4 cup plain, nonfat yogurt

White pepper to taste
1 pinch fresh ground nutmeg

1. Cook Penne noodles according to directions.
2. In a sauce pan melt butter. Add the fontina, gorgonzola, and boursin cheeses. Stir until melted.
3. Add parmesan, milk, and yogurt. Let simmer until slightly thickened.
4. Add sauce to hot, fresh-cooked noodles. Serve immediately. Top with nutmeg and freshly ground pepper.

Nutrition Information Per Serving

Calories 448	Fat 15 g	Fiber 10 g
Carbohydrates 58 g	Omega-3 Fats 944 mg	Calcium 304 mg
Protein 21 g	Cholesterol 32 mg	Sodium 538 mg

The Convenience of Casseroles

6

Casserole dishes are perhaps the most versatile of all meals. They can be simple Saturday night supper options that are sure to please the kids, like our Upside-Down Bacon Cheeseburger casserole, or they can be elegant enough to serve at an intimate candlelight dinner for two. Plain or fancy, they're even better when you add a little flax.

Cassoulet
Preparation time: 30 minutes
Cooking time: 3-1/2 hours
Yield: 12 cups

This dish takes long, slow cooking to bring out the complexity of its many flavors, but the end result is well worth the effort. You'll get rave reviews once family or friends sample this sophisticated French classic.

1 – 16 ounce bag dry navy beans
2 cups reduced sodium chicken broth
12 ounces raw chicken, skinless, boneless, cut in 1-inch pieces
4 ounces ham, cut into 1-inch pieces
2 medium carrots, peeled, 1/4-inch thick pieces
1 yellow onion, coarsely chopped
1 celery stalk, trimmed, sliced
2 tablespoons brown sugar
salt, to taste
1/8 teaspoon ground mustard
1/8 teaspoon black pepper
1 -14.5 ounce can diced tomatoes, with juice
1 tablespoon molasses

2 tablespoons ketchup
1/2 cup toasted flaxseed

1. Sort beans for small stones, rinse beans. Using the quick soak method, add beans to water in a large saucepan, and bring to a boil for 1-2 minutes. Take off heat and soak for 1 hour.
2. Drain off water, add the broth. Add all remaining ingredients except the flaxseed. Cover again and continue cooking on low heat another 2 to 2-1/2 hours or until the chicken is fully cooked and the beans are soft.
3. When the cassoulet mixture is ready to serve, fold in the toasted flaxseed, mixing thoroughly. Serve in a beautiful casserole dish for an impressive presentation at the table.

Nutrition Information Per Cup

Calories 242	Fat 5 g	Fiber 12 g
Carbohydrates 31 g	Omega-3 Fats 1893 mg	Calcium 112 mg
Protein 19 g	Cholesterol 22 mg	Sodium 352 mg

Almond Seafood Casserole
Preparation time: 15 minutes
Cooking time: 45 minutes
Yield: 4 servings

This is a surprisingly quick and easy meal that works equally well for a casual supper or served for a special occasion. The combination of textures and tastes make it a real crowd pleaser.

1 tablespoon extra virgin olive oil
1/4 cup bell pepper, chopped
1/4 cup celery, chopped
1/4 cup onion, chopped
2 cups brown rice, cooked
8 ounces frozen salad shrimp, thawed
½ cup imitation crab meat, shredded

1 - 8 ounce can water chestnuts, sliced and drained
1/3 cup light mayonnaise
1/2 cup V-8 juice
1/8 teaspoon white pepper

Topping
1/2 cup reduced fat cheddar cheese, shredded
1/4 cup slivered almonds, toasted
2 tablespoons toasted flaxseed

1. Preheat oven to 350 F.
2. Saute bell pepper, celery, and onion in skillet with olive oil. Take off heat.
3. Combine the brown rice, shrimp, crabmeat, water chestnuts, and vegetables in a large bowl. Moisten with the mayonnaise and V-8 juice, then add the white pepper and mix well.
4. Place into a casserole dish sprayed with non-stick spray.
5. In a separate bowl, mix cheese and slivered almonds, and sprinkle this topping evenly over the mixture.
6. Bake covered for approximately 35 minutes, until golden brown. Remove from oven, sprinkle on the toasted flaxseed, and serve hot.

Nutrition Information Per Serving

Calories 418	Fat 18 g	Fiber 5 g
Carbohydrates 35 g	Omega-3 Fats 1425 mg	Calcium 150 mg
Protein 28 g	Cholesterol 136 mg	Sodium 845 mg

Artichoke Chicken and Rice
Preparation time: 35 minutes
Cooking time: 60 minutes
Yield: 6 servings

Artichoke hearts are the secret to turning an old, familiar standby like chicken and rice into an elegant standout.

1 cup cooked brown rice
3/4 cup cooked wild rice
1 teaspoon unsalted butter
1 cup shredded carrots
1/4 cup bell pepper, chopped
2 tablespoons chopped green onion
1 - 10.75 ounce can cream of chicken soup, condensed
1/4 cup skim milk
2 tablespoons dry sherry(optional)
1 cup cooked chicken, boneless, skinless, cubed
1/2 cup reduced sodium chicken broth
1 cup part skim mozzarella cheese, shredded
1/3 cup ground flaxseed
1 – 13.75 ounce can regular artichoke hearts, drained and quartered
2 tablespoons grated Parmesan cheese
fresh parsley, finely minced, to garnish

1. Preheat oven to 350 F.
2. Prepare your wild and brown rice and combine them thoroughly. Set aside.
3. Melt butter in a large saucepan over medium heat, being careful not to let it turn brown. Add carrots, pepper, and green onions to the butter, and cook until the onions turn golden.
4. Add soup, milk, sherry, chicken, chicken broth, and mozzarella mixing well. Blend thoroughly, then remove saucepan from heat and stir in the ground flaxseed. Set aside.
5. Lightly grease an oven-proof casserole dish. Spread the mixture of wild and brown rice in the dish, forming an even layer. Arrange the artichoke hearts in a single layer on top of the rice. Pour the chicken-vegetable mixture over the artichokes.
6. Cover and bake for 35 to 40 minutes. Remove the cover, top with Parmesan cheese, and bake another 20 minutes or until the Parmesan topping turns golden brown. Sprinkle fresh parsley on top just before serving.

Nutrition Information Per Serving

Calories 269	Fat 11 g	Fiber 7 g
Carbohydrates 26 g	Omega-3 Fats 1757 mg	Calcium 203 mg
Protein 19 g	Cholesterol 36 mg	Sodium 723 mg

Asian Noodles w/ Chicken
Preparation time: 10 minutes
Cooking time: 20 minutes
Yield: 4 servings

If you buy your flax noodles ready made, this recipe can get you out of the kitchen and at the table in 30 minutes or less! If you're feeling overworked and overscheduled, the ease of preparation makes this a real time-saver. By the way, you can find stir-fry sauce in the ethnic foods section of your local supermarket.

8 ounces Hodgson Mill spaghetti flax noodles, dry
or homemade pasta (recipe, page 83)
1/2 teaspoon canola oil
1/4 teaspoon sesame oil
12 ounces boneless, skinless chicken breast, cut into strips
1 small red bell pepper, cut into slices
2 green onions, cut into slices
1/4 cup stir-fry sauce
1/4 teaspoon red pepper flakes
1 tablespoon fresh chopped cilantro
1 tablespoon toasted sesame seeds
2 tablespoons toasted flaxseed

1. Cook pasta, drain, and keep warm.
2. Heat the canola and sesame seed oil in a large skillet or wok over high heat. Quickly add the chicken and stir-fry approximately 5 minutes, until the chicken is thoroughly cooked.
3. Add pepper and onion strips to the pan and stir-fry for another 2 minutes. While still stirring, add sauce, red pepper flakes, and cilantro.

4. Mix the stir-fry with the cooked pasta and serve in an attractive dish. Garnish with toasted sesame and flax seeds. Serve hot.

Nutrition Information Per Serving

Calories 376	Fat 8 g	Fiber 10 g
Carbohydrates 45 g	Omega-3 Fats 2086 mg	Calcium 54 mg
Protein 30 g	Cholesterol 49 mg	Sodium 291 mg

Upside down Bacon Cheeseburger Casserole
Preparation time: 15 minutes
Cooking time: 45 minutes
Yield: 6 servings

You can call this a casserole or a savory pie. No matter what you call it, it's a real kid-pleaser, and adults love it too.

Filling
1 pound ground turkey
1 medium onion, sliced
1 medium bell pepper, cut into strips
6 slices turkey bacon, cooked, chopped
1 - 14 ounce can pizza sauce, chunky style
2 plum tomatoes, chopped
4 ounces reduced fat cheddar cheese, shredded

Crust
2 eggs
1 cup skim milk
1 tablespoon extra virgin olive oil
3/4 cup all-purpose flour
salt, to taste
1/8 teaspoon baking powder
1/4 cup ground flaxseed

1. Preheat oven to 400 F.

2. In a large saucepan, brown the turkey, then add onion slices and bell pepper. Cook until the vegetables are softened and the turkey meat is fully cooked.

3. Add chopped bacon and pizza sauce to turkey mixture. Stir until the mixture is thoroughly blended.

4. Coat a 9 X 13 casserole dish with non-stick spray. Pour mixture into casserole dish.

5. Add the chopped tomatoes to form a smooth layer, followed by a layer of cheese. Set casserole dish aside.

6. Place eggs in a medium mixing bowl and beat slightly. Add milk and oil, then mix in the flour, salt, baking powder, and flax, stirring until fully blended.

7. Pour the batter-like mixture over the top of the turkey mixture, spreading it to the edges of the casserole dish. Bake uncovered for 20 to 30 minutes, until the crust turns a rich, golden brown.

Nutrition Information Per Serving

Calories 367	Fat 18 g	Fiber 3 g
Carbohydrates 24 g	Omega-3 Fats 1420 mg	Calcium 228 mg
Protein 28 g	Cholesterol 143 mg	Sodium 803 mg

Chicken & Vegetable Stew
Preparation time: 20 minutes
Cooking time: 6 hours
Yield: 9 cups

This dish takes a long time to cook, but don't let that put you off, because all the work is done by your slow-cooker or crock-pot. That means you're only in the kitchen for the time it takes to put the ingredients together—20 minutes, tops! To add a touch of elegance, serve it on whole-wheat toast points.

1 medium onion, chopped
1 bell pepper, chopped
1 large carrot, peeled, cut into 1/4" slices
1 potato, with peel, cut into ½" dice

12 ounces skinless, boneless chicken, cut into 1" dice
1 – 15 ounce can garbanzo beans, drained and rinsed
1 – 15 ounce can tomato sauce
1 – 8 ounce can sliced mushrooms, drained
1/2 cup V-8 juice
1/4 cup toasted flaxseed

1. Place all ingredients, except the flaxseed, in a crock pot. Set the pot on low and let it cook for 6 hours.
2. Just before serving, toast slices of whole-wheat bread and cut into triangles. Place two triangles at the bottom of each serving bowl, and spoon up the stew. Garnish with toasted flaxseed.

Nutrition Information Per Cup

Calories 169	Fat 3 g	Fiber 6 g
Carbohydrates 22 g	Omega-3 Fats 1226 mg	Calcium 62 mg
Protein 15 g	Cholesterol 22 mg	Sodium 461 mg

Mexican Steak and Rice Casserole
Preparation time: 10 minutes
Cooking time: 40 minutes
Yield: 8 servings

These days just about everybody loves Mexican-style cooking, and because it is quick and easy to do, I think cooks love it most of all.

2 tablespoons extra virgin olive oil
16 ounces beef sirloin steak, cut into ½" cubes
1/2 cup chopped onions
3 tablespoons taco seasoning
1-1/2 cups instant rice, uncooked
3 cups water
1 – 15 ounce can red kidney beans, drained and rinsed
1 – 14.5 ounce can diced canned tomatoes
1 – 15 ounce can whole kernel corn, drained

1/4 teaspoon chili powder
1/4 cup ground flaxseed
1/4 cup reduced fat cheddar cheese, shredded

1. Preheat oven to 350 F and coat 2 quart casserole dish with non-stick spray.
2. Pour olive oil into a large saucepan and place over high heat.
3. Add beef cubes, turning them so that they brown evenly, about 4 minutes (2 minutes each side). During the last couple of minutes, add the chopped onions, so that they'll cook without crisping.
4. Add taco seasoning, rice, and water. When the mixture comes to a boil, cover skillet and reduce heat to simmer. Cook about 15 minutes, or until the rice is tender.
5. Remove rice and beef mixture from heat and stir in the kidney beans, tomatoes, chili powder, corn, and flaxseed. Pour into casserole dish and top with the shredded cheese.
6. Bake uncovered for 20 minutes, 350 F, or until cheese topping is melted.

Nutrition Information Per Serving

Calories 401	Fat 14 g	Fiber 6 g
Carbohydrates 48 g	Omega-3 Fats 1156 mg	Calcium 61 mg
Protein 19 g	Cholesterol 38 mg	Sodium 594 mg

Chicken Cacciatore
Preparation time: 20 minutes
Cooking time: 60 minutes
Yield: 6 servings

Here's another traditional casserole with a flaxseed twist. You'll find that the nutty flavor of the ground flaxseed makes a perfect counterpoint to the more conventional herbs and spices of this dish.

whole chicken, cut into 8 pieces, skinned
seasoned flour (recipe, page 56)

2 tablespoons extra virgin olive oil
1 medium green pepper, cut into 1-inch cubes
1 large onion, cut into 1-inch cubes
1 – 14.5 ounce can diced tomatoes
1 – 8 ounce can tomato sauce mixed with 8 oz water
1 cup fresh mushrooms, sliced
¼ cup ground flaxseed
1/2 teaspoon fresh oregano, chopped or leaf oregano
1/4 teaspoon fresh basil, chopped or leaf basil
salt, to taste
2 cloves garlic, chopped finely
1/4 cup grated Parmesan cheese

1. Rinse chicken pieces and dredge them in the seasoned flour until each piece is evenly coated. Set aside.
2. Heat the oil in a large saucepan over medium-high heat. Place chicken pieces into the oil, being careful to avoid splattering.
3. Cook uncovered approximately 20 minutes, until the chicken is golden brown.
4. Add peppers and onions to the saucepan and cook for another minute, then add in all the remaining ingredients, except Parmesan cheese.
5. Bring mixture to a boil, then reduce and simmer covered for another 30 to 40 minutes.
6. Garnish with Parmesan cheese and serve.

Nutrition Information Per Serving

Calories 194	Fat 9 g	Fiber 3 g
Carbohydrates 12 g	Omega-3 Fats 1363 mg	Calcium 111 mg
Protein 18 g	Cholesterol 36 mg	Sodium 496 mg

Chicken Divan
Preparation time: 10 minutes
Cooking time: 45 minutes
Yield: 6 servings

This dish can look pretty impressive, but it's surprisingly easy to make. And the sauce is so tasty that even kids have been known to eat their broccoli without complaints.

2 tablespoons unsalted butter
2 tablespoons all-purpose flour
2 tablespoons reduced sodium chicken bouillon, granulated
2 1/4 cups skim milk
1/3 cup light mayonnaise
1 tablespoon Dijon mustard
3 cups cooked skinless, boneless chicken, cubed
1 pound broccoli spears, fresh (blanched) or
frozen (thawed and drained)
1/2 cup reduced fat cheddar cheese, shredded
1/3 cup bread crumbs
1 tablespoon unsalted butter, melted
1/4 cup toasted whole flaxseed

1. Preheat oven to 350 F and spray 9 X13 baking pan with non-stick spray.
2. Melt butter in 3 quart saucepan over low heat.
3. Stir in flour and bouillon, then slowly add the milk and cook on medium heat, stirring frequently until thickened.
4. Add mayonnaise and mustard, blending well. Remove from heat and set aside.
5. In baking dish, arrange the chicken in an even layer, followed by a layer of broccoli. Pour sauce over the chicken and broccoli, and sprinkle the cheese over the top.
6. In a separate bowl, combine the bread crumbs, butter, and toasted flaxseed. Spread the mixture evenly over the top of the casserole, then bake uncovered for approximately 30-35 minutes.

Nutrition Information Per Serving

Calories 358	Fat 18 g	Fiber 5 g
Carbohydrates 16 g	Omega-3 Fats 1951 mg	Calcium 246 mg
Protein 32 g	Cholesterol 84 mg	Sodium 913 mg

Turkey Penne Casserole
Preparation time: 5 minutes
Cooking time: 35 minutes
Yield: 8 servings

Wondering what to do with the leftovers after a turkey dinner? This casserole makes a great change of pace from the usual turkey sandwiches!

8 ounces Hodgson Mill flax penne noodles, dry or
homemade pasta (recipe, page 83)
2 tablespoons unsalted butter
2 tablespoons all-purpose flour
salt, to taste
2 cups skim milk
1 cup reduced fat cheddar cheese, shredded
1 - 10 ounce package frozen peas
12 ounces cooked turkey, diced
basic flax breading (recipe, page 57)

1. Preheat oven to 350 F.
2. Cook pasta, drain, and set aside.
3. In a large saucepan, melt butter over low heat, then add flour and salt. Cook, stirring constantly, until the mixture is smooth and bubbly.
4. Remove from heat and gradually stir in milk.
5. Return saucepan to stovetop and heat to boiling, stirring constantly.
6. Add cheese and continue stirring until the cheese is melted. Remove from heat and set aside.

7. Combine the pasta with the peas, turkey, and sauce in an ungreased, 2-quart casserole, mixing them thoroughly. Sprinkle breading mixture on top. Bake uncovered for about 25 minutes or until hot and bubbly.

Nutrition Information Per Serving

Calories 358	Fat 12 g	Fiber 8 g
Carbohydrates 35 g	Omega-3 Fats 2336 mg	Calcium 207 mg
Protein 26 g	Cholesterol 48 mg	Sodium 364 mg

Jambalaya
Preparation time: 10 minutes
Cooking time: 30 minutes
Yield: 8 servings

There's nothing like a little taste of New Orleans to add pizzazz to your table. Jambalaya, whether its made the old-fashioned way or in our flax-enhanced version, is traditionally served with rice. We recommend brown rice, because that will maximize the nutritional value of this great dish. And by the way, our kitchen testers said that this dish tasted even better on the second day!

1/4 teaspoon black pepper
1/2 teaspoon garlic, finely chopped
12 ounces chicken breast, cut into 1/2-inch pieces
2 tablespoons extra virgin olive oil
1 cup onions, coarsely chopped
1 small bell pepper, coarsely chopped
1 stalk celery, coarsely chopped
4 ounces smoked sausage, cut into 1/2-inch slices
4 cups salsa or picante sauces
2 – 14.5 ounce cans Italian stewed tomatoes
1/2 cup water
2 cups uncooked brown rice
1 tablespoon hot sauce
1/4 cup toasted flaxseed

1. In large bowl, combine garlic and black pepper—roll the chicken pieces in the spices, making sure each piece is coated.
2. Heat oil in large, heavy skillet until hot, then add chicken pieces and cook at medium heat for about 5 minutes, until the chicken is thoroughly cooked.
3. Add onions, peppers, celery, and sausage, and cook for 5 minutes more. For more intense flavor, grill the chicken and sausage before hand.
4. Add stewed tomatoes, picante sauce (or salsa), water, rice, and hot sauce, reduce heat, and simmer the mixture for 20 minutes.
5. Remove from heat. Fold in toasted flaxseed.

Nutrition Information Per Serving

Calories 387	Fat 12 g	Fiber 7 g
Carbohydrates 52 g	Omega-3 Fats 1390 mg	Calcium 136 mg
Protein 19 g	Cholesterol 33 mg	Sodium 734 mg

Tetrazzini
Preparation time: 5 minutes
Cooking time: 50 minutes
Yield: 6 servings

Talk about versatility! Tetrazzini is a pasta dish that tastes great plain, but can be "dressed up" for company with the addition of chicken, turkey, or shrimp. No matter whether you go for the plain or the fancy versions, however, it's the flax noodles that give our take on this dish its distinctive flair.

8 ounce Hodgson Mill flax spaghetti noodles, dry, broken into pieces
or homemade pasta (recipe, page 83)
1/4 cup extra virgin olive oil
1/4 cup all-purpose flour
salt, to taste
1/4 teaspoon black pepper
1 – 14 ounce can reduced sodium chicken broth
1 cup skim milk

2 tablespoons dry sherry (optional)
4 ounces sliced mushrooms, canned or 1 cup fresh sliced mushrooms
2 cups cooked, diced chicken, turkey, or baby shrimp (optional)
1/2 cup Parmesan cheese, grated
1/4 cup toasted flaxseed

1. Preheat oven to 350 F.
2. Prepare spaghetti, drain, and set aside.
3. In a 3 quart sauce pan, blend oil and flour together with salt and pepper, and cook over low heat until bubbly, approximately 2 to 3 minutes.
4. Remove from heat and add broth and milk to pan. Return pan to heat (still set on low) and simmer for 2 minutes. If using fresh raw mushrooms, add now and cook for 2 more minutes. Remove from heat and set aside.
5. Combine spaghetti, sherry, cream sauce, and mushrooms (if using canned) with the sauce in a 9 X 13 casserole dish (sprayed with non-stick coating), mixing all ingredients thoroughly. If you're planning on adding chicken, turkey, or shrimp, add it now.
6. Top with Parmesan cheese and bake uncovered for 30 minutes.
7. Just before serving, top casserole with toasted flaxseed, or provide it at the table so that each diner can sprinkle it on for themselves.

Nutrition Information Per Serving

Calories 411	Fat 18 g	Fiber 7 g
Carbohydrates 34 g	Omega-3 Fats 2304 mg	Calcium 204 mg
Protein 28 g	Cholesterol 47 mg	Sodium 508 mg

Arroz Con Pollo
Preparation time: 5 minutes
Cooking time: 40 minutes
Yield: 4 servings

This classic Spanish dish adds a festive touch to any occasion. When you present this dish at your table, your fellow diners will say "Ole!"

1 tablespoon extra virgin olive oil
4 – 4 ounces boneless, skinless chicken breasts
1 large onion, chopped
1 cup uncooked white rice
1 teaspoon cumin
2-1/2 cups reduced sodium chicken broth
1/2 cup salsa
1 red or green bell pepper, chopped
1 cup frozen peas
1/4 cup ground flaxseed

1. Heat oil in large saucepan. Add chicken breast and saute about 5 to 7 minutes, until browned. Remove chicken from skillet and set aside.
2. Using the same oil, cook the chopped onions for approximately 4 minutes, until translucent and golden in color.
3. Add rice and cumin to the skillet, stirring to mix thoroughly. Add broth and salsa.
4. Bring mixture to a boil, then reduce heat to simmer and add chicken back into the pan. Cover and cook on low heat for 20 - 25 minutes, until rice and chicken are thoroughly cooked.
5. Stir in bell pepper, peas, and flaxseed and cook for 5 minutes more. Serve piping hot.

Nutrition Information Per Serving

Calories 435	Fat 9 g	Fiber 7 g
Carbohydrates 51 g	Omega-3 Fats 2025 mg	Calcium 74 mg
Protein 36 g	Cholesterol 66 mg	Sodium 560 mg

Garden Risotto
Preparation time: 20 minutes
Cooking time: 30 minutes
Yield: 6 servings

This is a great side dish frequently offered as a summertime treat. It's so tasty, however, that its fans will be glad to see it all year round. To make it extra creamy, try adding heavy cream at the same time that you add the broccoli and carrots.

1 tablespoon extra virgin olive oil
1/4 cup green onions, thinly sliced
1/4 cup chopped red bell peppers
1 cup Arborio rice, uncooked
1 – 14 ounce can vegetable broth
3/4 cup water
1 cup broccoli florets, fresh, chopped
1/2 cup shredded carrots
2 ounces heavy cream (optional)
1 teaspoon dried thyme leaves
1/4 cup toasted flaxseed
2 tablespooons fresh Parmesan cheese, shredded

1. In a large nonstick saucepan, heat oil over medium heat. Add onions, pepper, and rice and cook for 2 minutes.
2. Slowly add the broth, cover, reduce heat, and simmer uncovered for 10 minutes.
3. Slowly add the water, broccoli, and carrots, and simmer for 5-10 minutes until the vegetables are al dente. If you want the creamier sauce, add the heavy cream now, stirring to blend it in smoothly.
4. Remove from heat, then stir in thyme and flaxseed, and cover the pan. Let sit for 2 minutes for the mixture to "set" then top with Parmesan cheese and serve.

Nutrition Information Per Serving

Calories 194	Fat 6 g	Fiber 4 g
Carbohydrates 29 g	Omega-3 Fats 1821 mg	Calcium 54 mg
Protein 6 g	Cholesterol 1 mg	Sodium 942 mg

Tuna Noodle Casserole
Preparation time: 5 minutes
Cooking time: 45 minutes
Yield: 8 servings

Just about every household has a variant of this Saturday night standby. It's simple, it's quick, and it seems to please every tastebud. We're betting that once you try our flaxseed version, it will become your new family favorite.

1 – 10 ounce box Hodgson Mill flax spiral noodles, dry or
homemade pasta (recipe, page 83)
2 tablespoons unsalted butter
2 tablespoons all-purpose flour
salt, to taste
2 cups skim milk
1 cup reduced fat cheddar cheese, shredded
1/2 cup light sour cream
1 cup frozen peas
1 – 12 ounce can tuna, canned in water, drained
basic breading mixture (recipe, page 57)

1. Heat oven to 350 F.
2. Prepare pasta per directions, drain, and set aside.
3. In a 1-1/2 quart saucepan, combine butter, flour, and salt. Cook over low heat, stirring constantly until the mixture is smooth and bubbling.
4. Remove pan from heat and gradually stir in the milk. Return pan to stove and heat to boiling, stirring constantly, for 1 minute. Stir in cheese and cook until the cheese has melted. Remove from heat and fold in the sour cream.
5. In an ungreased 2-quart casserole, combine pasta, peas, tuna and the sauce, mixing all ingredients thoroughly. Sprinkle breading mixture evenly over the top. Bake uncovered for about 25 minutes, until sauce is bubbling and the topping is golden brown.

Nutrition Information Per Serving

Calories 355	Fat 11 g	Fiber 8 g
Carbohydrates 38 g	Omega-3 Fats 2524 mg	Calcium 208 mg
Protein 25 g	Cholesterol 30 mg	Sodium 352 mg

A Tribute to John Montague, Earl of Sandwich

7

You may be wondering just who was John Montague and what is he doing in this book. John Montague was a member of the British aristocracy, the fourth Earl of Sandwich, who, according to legend, became addicted to gambling at cards. So avid was he in his gaming that he wouldn't leave the card table for anything, not even for meals. He is said to have demanded that meat and bread be brought to him, and to have slapped them together to make a convenient meal that he could eat without taking his eyes off the cards. Thus was born the meal that bears his name today, or so the story goes. There is more than a little doubt that the legend is true.

Whoever invented the sandwich, what's plain is that we've gotten creative over time, coming up with a wide variety of tasty fillings. And when you add flax, you end up with a nutrient-dense alternative to more traditional sandwich fare. Let's start off with a couple of variations on that most basic of all sandwich fillings: peanut butter.

Homemade Flax-Enriched Nut Butter
Preparation time: 5 minutes
Yield: 2 cups

1-16 ounce jar unsalted dry roasted peanuts
4 tablespoons ground flaxseed

1. Put unsalted peanuts in a food processor and blend on medium, until mixture becomes liquidy (3-4 minutes).

2. Add ground flaxseed and continue processing just until blended(15-30 seconds). Consistency should be liquid enough to pour into a storage container.
3. If is a bit dry, add a small amount of your favorite oil(canola or extra-virgin olive oil preferred). Refrigerate until needed. Storing in refrigerator for up 2 weeks will be safe. Freezing is not recommended.

Nutrition Information Per Tablespoon

Calories 88	Fat 8 g	Fiber 1 g
Carbohydrates 3 g	Omega-3 Fats 242 mg	Calcium 10 mg
Protein 4 g	Cholesterol 0 mg	Sodium 1 mg

Honey Peanut Butter
Preparation time: 5 minutes
Yield: 2 ¼ cups

1 – 16 ounce jar unsalted dry roasted peanuts
4 tablespoons ground flaxseed
¼ - 1/2 cup honey(depends on your taste)

1. Put unsalted peanuts in a food processor and blend on medium,until mixture becomes liquidy(about 3-4 minutes).
2. Add ground flaxseed and honey, continue processing just until blended (30-45 seconds). Consistency should be liquid enough to pour into a storage container.
3. Refrigerate until needed. Storing in refrigerator for up 2 weeks will be safe. Freezing is not recommended.

Nutrition Information Per Tablespoon

Calories 85	Fat 7 g	Fiber 1 g
Carbohydrates 5 g	Omega-3 Fats 215 mg	Calcium 9 mg
Protein 3 g	Cholesterol 0 mg	Sodium 1 mg

Our creativity isn't limited to what we put into the middle of our sandwiches. We've got all sorts of options for the outside too, from buns and wraps to pita bread. And the most recent wrinkle on the Earl of Sandwich's invention is Panini. In the pages that follow, you'll find plenty of options for your pleasure.

Turkey Club Saute

Preparation time: 12 minutes
Cooking time: 10 minutes
Yield: 1 serving

3 ounces raw turkey breast, slightly pounded
Basic flax breading (recipe, page 57)
1-2 teaspoons extra virgin olive oil
2 slices tomato
2 slices bacon, cooked
2 lettuce leaves
2 slices thick, whole grain bread, toasted

1. Bread turkey breast with basic flax breading.
2. In skillet, saute turkey breast in olive oil until done, about 4-5 minutes on each side.
3. Place on 1 slice of bread, top with tomato, bacon, and lettuce.
4. Top with other slice of bread and serve.

Nutrition Information

Calories 384	Fat 15 g	Fiber 6 g
Carbohydrates 30 g	Omega-3 Fats 1602 mg	Calcium 96 mg
Protein 32 g	Cholesterol 62 mg	Sodium 518 mg

Ground Turkey Burger

Preparation time: 5 minutes
Cooking time: 8-10 minutes
Yield: 4 servings

1 pound ground turkey
1/2 cup diced onions
1/4 cup ground flaxseed
2 tablespoons Worcestershire Sauce
1/4 teaspoon black pepper
salt, to taste
1/4 cup water
4 whole wheat buns

1. In a bowl, mix all ingredients together(except buns), kneading them by hand until thoroughly blended.
2. Separate into four equal portions and form each portion into patties ½ " thick. Grill to an internal temperature of 165 F or until well done.
3. Serve on whole-wheat buns.

Nutrition Information Per Serving

Calories 333	Fat 15 g	Fiber 6 g
Carbohydrates 25 g	Omega-3 Fats 2107 mg	Calcium 92 mg
Protein 26 g	Cholesterol 90 mg	Sodium 433 mg

Salmon Burger
Preparation time: 10 minutes
Cooking time: 15 minutes
Yield: 4 servings

1 – 14.75 ounce can salmon, drained
1/4 cup red onions, diced
1/4 cup ground flaxseed
2 tablespoons Worcestershire Sauce
1/4 teaspoon black pepper
1 egg
1/4 cup plain bread crumbs
4 whole wheat buns

1. Mix all ingredients in bowl (except buns), kneading the mixture by hand until everything is well blended.
2. Form into four equal sized patties, about 3/4-inches thick, and about 3-4 inches in diameter.
3. Grill to an internal temperature of 160 F, or until well done.
4. Serve on toasted buns.

Nutrition Information Per Serving

Calories 327	Fat 11 g	Fiber 6 g
Carbohydrates 29 g	Omega-3 Fats 3182 mg	Calcium 110 mg
Protein 29 g	Cholesterol 108 mg	Sodium 470 mg

Southwestern Chicken
Preparation time: 15 minutes
Cooking time: 15 minutes
Yield: 1 serving

4 ounce boneless, skinless chicken breast
2 tablespoons southwestern flax breading (recipe, page 57)
1-2 teaspoon unsalted butter
2 tablespoons pico de gallo
1 slice pepper jack cheese
1 whole wheat bun

1. Coat chicken breast with breading mix.
2. In skillet, saute chicken breast in butter till done, about 5 minutes on each side.
3. Top with pico de gallo, then cheese. Cover pan with lid until cheese is melted.
4. Remove from pan and serve on bun.

Nutrition Information Per Serving

Calories 417	Fat 17 g	Fiber 5 g
Carbohydrates 26 g	Omega-3 Fats 1436 mg	Calcium 287 mg
Protein 40 g	Cholesterol 101 mg	Sodium 853 mg

Barbequed Pork
Preparation time: 10 minutes
Cooking time: 15 minutes
Yield: 4 servings

1 teaspoon unsalted butter
1 cup minced onion
1/4 teaspoon dry mustard
1 pound precooked barbequed pork in sauce
3 tablespoons toasted flaxseed
4 slices tomato
4 slices low-fat cheddar cheese
4 whole wheat buns

1. In a large saucepan, add butter and minced onion, cook until tender, approximately 5 minutes.
2. Add dry mustard and blend well.
3. Add precooked pork, and heat thoroughly over medium heat.
4. Add flax and remove from heat.
5. Portion evenly onto 4 buns, top with cheese and tomato. Serve hot.

Nutrition Information Per Serving

Calories 439	Fat 18 g	Fiber 6 g
Carbohydrates 27 g	Omega-3 Fats 1999 mg	Calcium 151 mg
Protein 42 g	Cholesterol 98 mg	Sodium 554 mg

Loose Meat Sandwich
Preparation time: 10 minutes
Cooking time: 20 minutes
Yield: 4 servings

1 pound ground turkey
1/2 cup diced onions
1 cup Cola, regular
1/4 cup water

1/4 cup ground flaxseed
2 tablespoons Worcestershire Sauce
1/8 teaspoon red pepper sauce
salt, to taste
4 whole wheat buns

1. In large saucepan, cook turkey and onions until brown.
2. Add remaining ingredients(except buns),cover, and cook over low heat for approximately 10-15 minutes until meat is well done.
3. Serve on whole wheat buns.

Nutrition Information Per Serving

Calories 338	Fat 15 g	Fiber 5 g
Carbohydrates 28 g	Omega-3 Fats 2099 mg	Calcium 84 mg
Protein 25 g	Cholesterol 90 mg	Sodium 400 mg

Sloppy Joes
Preparation time: 10 minutes
Cooking time: 25 minutes
Yield: 4 servings

1 pound ground turkey
1/2 cup diced onions
1/3 cup minced celery
1/3 cup chopped green peppers
1/2 cup barbeque sauce
1/4 cup water
1/4 cup ground flaxseed
1 tablespoon Worcestershire Sauce
1/4 teaspoon red pepper sauce
salt, to taste
1/2 teaspoon black pepper
4 whole wheat buns

1. In a large saucepan, cook turkey, onions, and celery until brown.

2. Add remaining ingredients(except buns), cover, and cook over low heat for approximately 10-15 minutes, until meat is well done.
3. Serve on hamburger buns.

Nutrition Information Per Serving

Calories 360	Fat 15 g	Fiber 7 g
Carbohydrates 30 g	Omega-3 Fats 2109 mg	Calcium 100 mg
Protein 26 g	Cholesterol 90 mg	Sodium 638 mg

Turkey Avocado Wrap
Preparation time: 10 minutes
Yield: 1 serving

1 flour tortilla, 7 inches in diameter
2 ounces sliced turkey
2 slices avocado
1 tablespoon herbed low-fat mayonnaise(or plain low-fat mayo w/ your favorite herbs)
1 tablespoon toasted flaxseed
2 slices tomato
Red onion, sliced and alfalfa sprouts, to taste

Layer ingredients in tortilla and fold. Cut, if desired.

Nutrition Information Per Serving

Calories 362	Fat 20 g	Fiber 5 g
Carbohydrates 22 g	Omega-3 Fats 2650 mg	Calcium 68 mg
Protein 23 g	Cholesterol 41 mg	Sodium 243 mg

Stuffed Pita
Preparation time: 35 minutes
Yield: 4 servings

4 ounces herbed feta cheese, crumbled
6 ounces chick peas, drained
4 ounces low calorie Italian dressing
2 tablespoons flax oil
1 teaspoon fresh lemon juice
2 tablespoons toasted flaxseed
1 whole tomato, diced
1/2 cup cucumber, peeled, seeds removed, diced
1/4 cup red onion, diced
2 pocket pita, whole wheat
4 romaine lettuce leaves

1. Combine all ingredients, except for pita and lettuce, in bowl. Let marinate covered for 30 minutes in refrigerator.
2. Cut pita bread in half. Place lettuce inside pita bread and 1/4 filling.

Nutrition Information Per Serving

Calories 323	Fat 18 g	Fiber 8 g
Carbohydrates 31 g	Omega-3 Fats 5383 mg	Calcium 187 mg
Protein 12 g	Cholesterol 25 mg	Sodium 672 mg

Cuban Sandwich
Preparation time: 30 minutes
Cooking time: 20 minutes
Yield: 4 servings

8 - 1 ounce slices roasted pork loin, prepared
as directed below.
4 - 1 ounce slices lean ham
4 dill pickle slices
4 - 1 ounce slices swiss cheese
4 French bread rolls or French bread cut into 6 inch sections
Mustard spread (see Panini section, below)

Marinade for pork loin
½ cup orange juice
4 tablespoons extra virgin olive oil
1 tablespoon lime juice
1 teaspoon garlic, chopped finely
1 teaspoon fresh cilantro, chopped finely
1 tablespoon brown sugar

Preparation of pork loin
1. In small bowl, mix all marinade ingredients together.
2. In large bowl, pour marinade over 1 pound pork roast.
3. Let rest in refrigerator for 4 hours, turning meat (about 2-3 times) to make certain meat is well coated.
4. Remove from marinade, pat dry.
5. Place in open roasting pan, roast at 350 F for about 1 hour or until done (center is 160 F).
6. Let cool and slice for use in sandwiches.

Creating the sandwich
1. Assemble the sandwich with 2 slices of pork, 1 slice of cheese and ham, 1 slice of pickle, with the French bread that has been lightly spread with mustard spread.
2. Grill on a hinged panini grill or in a pan or on a broiler. You may need to brush with butter before cooking. About 1-2 min on each side. Serve hot.

Nutrition Information Per Serving

Calories 448	Fat 24 g	Fiber 3 g
Carbohydrates 22 g	Omega-3 Fats 2100 mg	Calcium 340 mg
Protein 35 g	Cholesterol 87 mg	Sodium 868 mg

Paninis For One

And let's not forget the latest variation on the sandwich theme—those wonderful open-faced paninis! The classic panini is created on focaccia, but you can use any dense, crusty bread, from French baguettes to artisan bread. It's the spread that makes these sandwich alternatives truly special, and we've got a bunch of tasty flax-based options for you to try. We've provided recipes for single paninis, but you can make many of these spreads in larger quantities and have them ready for whenever you're looking for a special treat.

How to grill for panini

1. Brush small amount of softened or melted butter on outside of bread(of your choice).
2. Fill with sandwich ingredients and 2 tablespoons spread of choice.
3. Grill in hinged panini grill or any brand of grill or sandwich maker. Grill until ingredients are hot, about 1-2 minutes.

The Spreadables

Mustard
Preparation time: 5 minutes
Yield: 8 tablespoons

4 tablespoons Dijon Mustard or stone ground mustard
¼ cup ground flax
1 tablespoon flax oil
1 teaspoon white wine vinegar

Asiago
Preparation time: 5 minutes
Yield: 8 tablespoons

4 tablespoons asiago cheese, shredded
4 tablespoons low-fat mayonnaise
¼ cup ground flax
1 tablespoon low calorie Caesar dressing

Southwest Mayo
Preparation time: 5 minutes
Yield: 9 tablespoons

4 tablespoons low-fat mayonnaise
1 tablespoon sun dried tomatoes, minced
¼ cup ground flax
pinch cayenne pepper
1 tablespoon tomato pureed (fresh or canned)
salt and pepper to taste
1/4 teaspoon minced garlic
1 tablespoon diced chilies

Remember, you are limited only by your imagination when it comes to panini spreads. For instance, our classic pesto sauce, in Chapter 5, works really well for panini!

To Make it More of a Meal:

Sandwiches can be filling enough to make a meal in themselves, without adding much in way of preparation time. This comes in handy when we're only cooking for ourselves, and want something quick and easy and don't want to bother with leftovers. Here are some single-serving recipes that are truly convenient—not one of them will take more than 10 minutes to put together.

Beef and Cheese
2 ounces beef, thinly sliced
1 ounce provolone cheese
1 slice red onion
Mustard spread
Bread of choice

Nutrition Information

Calories 497	Fat 25 g	Fiber 5 g
Carbohydrates 35 g	Omega-3 Fats 4064 mg	Calcium 304 mg
Protein 32 g	Cholesterol 75 mg	Sodium 868 mg

Chicken and Spinach

3 ounces chicken breast, cooked, skinless, sliced
1/4 cup spinach leaves
Asiago spread
Bread of choice

Nutrition Information

Calories 467	Fat 19 g	Fiber 5 g
Carbohydrates 36 g	Omega-3 Fats 2003 mg	Calcium 164 mg
Protein 36 g	Cholesterol 94 mg	Sodium 838 mg

Turkey-Artichoke Combo

3 ounces roasted turkey, sliced
Asiago spread
1/4 cup spinach leaves, chopped
1/4 cup artichoke hearts, chopped
Bread of choice

1. Blend together spread, spinach leaves, and artichoke in a small bowl.
2. Spread on bread, top with turkey, top slice of bread.

Nutrition Information

Calories 498	Fat 19 g	Fiber 5 g
Carbohydrates 42 g	Omega-3 Fats 2003 mg	Calcium 173 mg
Protein 36 g	Cholesterol 81 mg	Sodium 832 mg

Southwestern Chicken

2 ounces thinly sliced chicken
1 ounce provolone cheese
2 tomato slices
1 slice red onion
Southwest mayo spread
Bread of choice

Nutrition Information

Calories 417	Fat 17 g	Fiber 5 g
Carbohydrates 26 g	Omega-3 Fats 1436 mg	Calcium 287 mg
Protein 40 g	Cholesterol 101 mg	Sodium 853 mg

Pizza Panini
1 ounce pepperoni
1 tablespoon red onion, minced
1 tablespoon green peppers, diced
1 ounce slice part skim mozzarella cheese
1 tablespoon pizza sauce
Pesto spread
Bread of choice

Nutrition Information

Calories 510	Fat 30 g	Fiber 5 g
Carbohydrates 38 g	Omega-3 Fats 2055 mg	Calcium 280 mg
Protein 21 g	Cholesterol 51 mg	Sodium 1202 mg

Italian
1/2 ounce Prosciutto
1 ounce provolone cheese
1/8 cup artichoke hearts (drained and sliced)
1/ 8 cup portabello mushrooms, sliced
Southwest mayo
Bread of choice

Nutrition Information

Calories 429	Fat 22 g	Fiber 4 g
Carbohydrates 38 g	Omega-3 Fats 1830 mg	Calcium 285 mg
Protein 19 g	Cholesterol 40 mg	Sodium 1110 mg

Ham and Cheese

2 ounces ham (thinly sliced)
1 ounce Swiss cheese
2 tablespoons sprouts of choice
Mustard spread
Bread of choice

Nutrition Information

Calories 486	Fat 25 g	Fiber 4 g
Carbohydrates 35 g	Omega-3 Fats 4114 mg	Calcium 362 mg
Protein 30 g	Cholesterol 68 mg	Sodium 1408 mg

Roasted Veggie

1/8 cup grilled portabella mushroom
1/8 cup grilled zucchini
1/8 cup mixed roasted red and yellow peppers (see below)
1/8 cup grilled tomato wedges
1 ounce part skim mozzarella cheese slice
Pesto spread
Bread of choice

Place whole red and yellow peppers directly over an open flame, turning occasionally. When the outside skin turns black, remove from flame and allow to cool. Cut in half, scrape off the blackened skin, and remove seeds, then slice thinly.

Nutrition Information

Calories 370	Fat 18 g	Fiber 5 g
Carbohydrates 37 g	Omega-3 Fats 2062 mg	Calcium 277 mg
Protein 16 g	Cholesterol 28 mg	Sodium 544 mg

Artichoke and Cheese

1 ounce provolone cheese
1 tablespoon asiago cheese
1 ounce part skim mozzarella cheese slice
1 tablespoon parmesan cheese
1/4 cup artichoke hearts (drained and sliced)
1 tablespoon red onion, minced
Asiago spread
Bread of choice

Nutrition Information

Calories 489	Fat 26 g	Fiber 5 g
Carbohydrates 43 g	Omega-3 Fats 2056 mg	Calcium 468 mg
Protein 21 g	Cholesterol 50 mg	Sodium 865 mg

Mozzarella and Olive

1 ounce part skim Mozzarella cheese slice
2 tablespoons black olives, sliced
2 tablespoons roasted red peppers, sliced
1 ounce reduced fat cheddar cheese slice
Asiago spread
Bread of choice

Nutrition Information

Calories 432	Fat 24 g	Fiber 5 g
Carbohydrates 37 g	Omega-3 Fats 2053 mg	Calcium 333 mg
Protein 16 g	Cholesterol 45 mg	Sodium 783 mg

Chicken Pesto
2 ounces sliced chicken breast
1 ounce fontina cheese
1 tablespoon black olives, sliced
1 tablespoon roasted red peppers, sliced
Pesto spread
Bread of choice

Nutrition Information

Calories 494	Fat 25 g	Fiber 5 g
Carbohydrates 34 g	Omega-3 Fats 2239 mg	Calcium 257 mg
Protein 33 g	Cholesterol 93 mg	Sodium 841 mg

Comfort Foods from the Flax-Friendly Kitchen

8

When you're down and feeling blue, nothing helps turn our mood around like a retreat to the foods that we associate with childhood—those wonderful comfort foods. We each have our own particular favorites, but certain dishes turn up on just about everybody's list. Here are a few that we've enhanced with a touch of flax!

Meatloaf
Preparation time: 15 minutes
Cooking time: 1 hour
Yield: 14 slices

Topping nearly everyone's list of comfort foods is the traditional meatloaf, just like mom used to make. It's a great candidate for flax-enhancement, too, because the flaxseed mixes so well with the rest of the mixture. Here's our take on this grand old dish.

2 slices whole wheat bread
1/2 cup ground flaxseed
1 large carrot, peeled and sliced
1 celery stalk, trimmed, chopped
1/2 medium onion, chopped
2 cloves fresh garlic, chopped
1/2 cup fresh parsley, finely minced
3/4 cup ketchup
1-1/2 tablespoons ground mustard
1 pound ground turkey
8 ounces lean ground beef
2 large eggs

salt, to taste
1 teaspoon pepper
1 teaspoon Tabasco sauce
1/2 teaspoon leaf rosemary
2 tablespoons dark brown sugar

1. Preheat oven to 375 F.
2. Remove crust from bread, put bread in food processer until fine.
3. Pour bread crumbs in large mixing bowl and blend in flaxseed.
4. Place carrots, celery, onion, garlic, parsley in food processor and blend until finely minced.
5. Add vegetables to bread crumb mixture and stir in well.
6. Add ½ cup ketchup, 1 tablespoon mustard, turkey, beef, eggs, salt, pepper, tabasco sauce, and rosemary.
7. Knead together until well blended.
8. Form into loaf and place in loaf pan (coated with non-stick spray).
9. Place remaining ketchup, mustard and brown sugar in small bowl and mix well.
10. Pour over top of meatloaf.
11. Bake at 375 F for 45 minutes to 1 hour, or until internal temperature is 160 F.

Nutrition Information Per Slice

Calories 138	Fat 7 g	Fiber 2 g
Carbohydrates 8 g	Omega-3 Fats 1157 mg	Calcium 36 mg
Protein 12 g	Cholesterol 66 mg	Sodium 228 mg

Chicken and Dumplings
Preparation time: 30 minutes
Cooking time: 2 hours 15 minutes
Yield: 4 servings

Running a close second to meatloaf is the stick-to-your-ribs savory pleasure of classic chicken and dumplings. We stick to tradition for the chicken stew that forms the backbone of the dish, but we enhance the dumplings with flax.

1 whole chicken, cut in 8 pieces
4 cups reduced sodium chicken broth
1 large onion, sliced
2 stalks celery, trimmed, cut into 1-inch pieces
1 bay leaf
1/4 teaspoon black pepper
1/2 cup all-purpose flour
3/4 cup cold water
1 – 16 ounce package frozen mixed vegetables

Dumplings

1/4 cup all-purpose flour
1/4 cup whole wheat flour
1 ½ tablespoons unsalted butter
1 teaspoon baking powder
1/4 cup ground flaxseed
1/3 cup skim milk

1. In large sauce pan, place chicken, broth, onion, celery, bay leaf, and pepper.
2. Simmer until chicken is tender, about 1-1 ½ hours.
3. Remove chicken from stock. Pull chicken off of bone, discarding bone and skin.
4. Strain the liquid and skim fat off top of liquid.
5. In a bowl, make a slurry with the water and flour, using a fork.
6. Stir into broth. Heat mixture until it boils and thickens, stirring constantly.
7. Add mixed vegetables and chicken back into mixture.
8. Place both the all-purpose and wheat flours in medium bowl. Cut butter into flour until it forms walnut-sized pieces.
9. Add remaining dry ingredients, stirring to blend them thoroughly.
10. Gradually add milk, stirring as you go.
11. Using a tablespoon or cookie scoop, drop portions of the dumpling dough onto the hot mixture. Cover and simmer gently for 15 minutes.

Nutrition Information Per Serving

Calories 358	Fat 10 g	Fiber 9 g
Carbohydrates 45 g	Omega-3 Fats 2115 mg	Calcium 171 mg
Protein 24 g	Cholesterol 47 mg	Sodium 816 mg

Chicken Pot Pie
Preparation time: 5 minutes
Cooking time: 2 hours
Yield: 4 servings

When the weather turns cold or rainy, and you want something warm and comforting, nothing does the trick like an old-fashioned pot pie. Here's our flax-enhanced version.

1 whole chicken, cut in 8 pieces
4 cups reduced sodium chicken broth
1 large onion, sliced
2 stalks celery, cut into 1-inch pieces
1 bay leaf
1/4 teaspoon black pepper
1/4 cup all-purpose flour
1/2 cup cold water
1 – 16 ounce package frozen mixed vegetables
1/4 cup ground flaxseed
1 pie crust

1. Preheat oven to 350 F.
2. In large sauce pan, place chicken, broth, onion, celery, bay leaf, and pepper.
3. Simmer until chicken is tender, about 1 to 1-1/2 hour.
4. Remove chicken from stock. Pull chicken off of bone, discarding bone and skin.
5. Strain the liquid and skim fat off top of liquid.
6. In a bowl, make a slurry with water and flour, using a fork.

7. Stir into broth. Heat mixture until it boils and thickens, stirring constantly.

8. Add mixed vegetables, chicken, and flax back into mixture.

9. Place mixture into 4 individual baking dishes (coated with non-stick spray).

10. Cut pie crust into 4 pieces and roll to desired shape, top baking dish.

11. Bake at 350 F till golden brown, approximately 30-40 minutes.

Nutrition Information Per Serving

Calories 391	Fat 16 g	Fiber 8 g
Carbohydrates 42 g	Omega-3 Fats 2313 mg	Calcium 77 mg
Protein 22 g	Cholesterol 35 mg	Sodium 887 mg

Shepherd's Pie
Preparation time: 10 minutes
Cooking time: 50 minutes
Yield: 8 servings

Ever wonder why certain foods become "comfort" foods? Because they're the foods we loved as kids. Here's our take on that great old standby, Shepherd's Pie, with a healthful twist. In place of ground beef we've gone with lower-fat turkey, and of course we've included a generous dollop of flax!

Filling
1-1/2 pounds ground turkey
salt, to taste
1-1/2 teaspoon black pepper
2 tablespoons unsalted butter
1 large onion, minced
2 carrots, peeled and sliced
1 teaspoon garlic, minced
2 tablespoons ketchup
3 cups reduced sodium chicken broth
1/4 cup red wine (optional)
1 teaspoon Worcestershire sauce
1 teaspoon ground thyme

1 teaspoon leaf rosemary
1 cup frozen peas
6 tablespoons ground flaxseed

Topping
2 pounds peeled russet potatoes, cut into 2-inch cubes
salt and pepper, to taste
4 tablespoons unsalted butter
3/4 cup skim milk
2 large eggs

1. Preheat oven to 400 F.
2. Brown turkey in large skillet, until well done.
3. Add salt and pepper. Place ground turkey in bowl, and set aside.
4. Place butter in saucepan, over medium heat. Add onions and carrots. Cook until tender.
5. Add garlic, and cook for 1 minute.
6. Add the remaining ingredients, except flax and peas. Bring to simmer, and add ground turkey. Cook uncovered for 15 minutes.
7. Fold in flax and peas, and remove from heat.
8. In a separate pot, cover potatoes with water, add salt, and bring to a boil.
9. Cook potatoes until tender, drain potatoes, and put back in pot. On low heat, mash potatoes, adding butter and warm milk. Blend well, add eggs.
10. Adjust seasonings.
11. Pour turkey mixture in 9 X 13 baking dish (coated with non-stick spray).
12. Spread mashed potatoes evenly on turkey mixture, making sure that no filling is showing.
13. Bake uncovered for 20 minutes. Let stand for about 5 minutes before serving.

Nutrition Information Per Serving

Calories 378	Fat 20 g	Fiber 6 g
Carbohydrates 27 g	Omega-3 Fats 1675 mg	Calcium 91 mg
Protein 23 g	Cholesterol 144 mg	Sodium 408 mg

Beef Stew

Preparation time: 10 minutes
Cooking time: 1-1/4 hours
Yield: 8 servings

Finally, what list of comfort foods would be complete without that cold-weather favorite, classic beef stew? Served in generous, steaming bowls, with crusty bread (flax-based, perhaps?) on the side, you've got a hearty meal that will warm you through the most bitter winter blizzards.

2 pounds chuck roast, cubed
salt and pepper, to taste
3 tablespoons extra virgin olive oil
1 large onion, chopped
3 cloves garlic, minced
1 cup red wine (optional)
2 cups reduced sodium beef broth
2 bay leaves
1 teaspoon ground thyme
1-1/2 pounds red potatoes, cut into 1-inch cubes
1 pound baby carrots
1 cup peas, frozen
¼ cup ground flaxseed

1. Preheat oven to 350 F.
2. In dutch oven or large roasting pan, over medium-high heat, add 2 tablespoons olive oil and seasoned beef. Stir until well browned. Remove and set aside.
3. Add remaining olive oil to dutch oven, add onion, and cook until tender about 5 minutes. Add garlic, cook 1 minute, add wine to deglaze the dutch oven.

4. Add remaining ingredients, including chuck roast, except for peas and flaxseed.

5. Cover pan and place in 350 F oven. Cook for 1 hour.

6. Remove from oven, fold in flax and peas, let stand 5 minutes. Remove bay leaves and serve.

Nutrition Information Per Serving

Calories 368	Fat 14 g	Fiber 5 g
Carbohydrates 23 g	Omega-3 Fats 1068 mg	Calcium 52 mg
Protein 37 g	Cholesterol 82 mg	Sodium 241 mg

Making the Most of Main Dishes

9

The versatility of flax means that it fits comfortably into any main dish. All it takes is a clever cook! We're hoping that the variety of kitchen-tested recipes offered here will tempt your taste-buds. Even more, we're hoping that once you've seen how easy it is to incorporate flax into these recipes, you'll be inspired to come up with ideas of your own! So, without further ado, let's get right to work!

SEAFOOD

Seafood Topped with sauteed vegetables
Preparation time: 15 minutes
Cooking time: 25 minutes
Yield: 4 servings

4 fillets flounder, orange roughy, or cod(4 ounces each)
egg wash (recipe, page 56)
basic flax breading (recipe, page 57)
1-2 tablespoons extra virgin olive oil
1/2 cup onions, sliced
1/2 cup sliced bell peppers (red, green, and yellow)
½ cup sliced mushrooms
2 teaspoons minced garlic
salt, to taste
1/4 teaspoon black pepper

1. Preheat oven to 350 F.
2. Dip fish in egg wash.

3. Coat with basic breading mixture.
4. Place on baking pan coated with non-stick spray.
5. Bake uncovered in preheated 350 F for 15-20 minutes.
6. In large skillet, saute vegetables in olive oil for 5 minutes, or until tender.
7. Add seasoning to vegetables.
8. Place fish on plate with 1/4 sauteed vegetable mixture.

Nutrition Information Per Serving

Calories 237	Fat 10 g	Fiber 4 g
Carbohydrates 11 g	Omega-3 Fats 2543 mg	Calcium 90 mg
Protein 26 g	Cholesterol 54 mg	Sodium 189 mg

Coconut Shrimp
Preparation time: 10 minutes
Cooking time: 15 minutes
Yield: 5 servings

1 pound large shrimp (16-20 pieces), peeled and deveined
seasoned flour (recipe, page 56)
egg wash (recipe, page 56)
coconut flax breading (recipe, page 58)
¼ - 1/3 cup canola oil
1/2 cup orange marmalade
1/4 cup Dijon mustard

1. Dredge shrimp in seasoned flour.
2. Dip shrimp in egg wash.
3. Bread with coconut flax breading.
4. Deep fry in canola oil until golden brown .
5. Blend marmalade and mustard together for dipping sauce.

Nutrition Information Per Serving

Calories 402	Fat 20 g	Fiber 3 g
Carbohydrates 35 g	Omega-3 Fats 3054 mg	Calcium 115 mg
Protein 22 g	Cholesterol 138 mg	Sodium 428 mg

Pecan Salmon
Preparation time: 10 minutes
Cooking time: 15 minutes
Yield: 4 servings

4 salmon fillets (4-6 ounces each)
salt and pepper, to taste
1-2 tablespoons extra virgin olive oil
pecan flax breading (recipe, page 57)

Remoulade sauce
½ cup low-fat mayonnaise
1 tablespoon Dijon mustard
1 teaspoon capers, chopped
½ teaspoon Italian seasoning

1. Preheat oven to 350 F.
2. Season salmon with salt and pepper.
3. Place in 9 X 13 roasting pan, which has been coated with non-stick spray.
4. Brush with olive oil.
5. Top with pecan breading mix.
6. Bake uncovered in 350 F for approximately 15 minutes, or till light and flaky.
7. Serve with remoulade sauce.

Nutrition Information Per Serving

Calories 406	Fat 29 g	Fiber 4 g
Carbohydrates 10 g	Omega-3 Fats 4874 mg	Calcium 71 mg
Protein 27 g	Cholesterol 62 mg	Sodium 409 mg

Flax Dusted White Fish
Preparation time: 5 minutes
Cooking time: 5 minutes
Yield: 4 servings

4 white fish fillets (4-6 ounces each)
salt and pepper, to taste
basic flax breading (recipe, page 57)
1-2 tablespoons unsalted butter

1. Season fish fillets with salt and pepper to taste.
2. Dredge in basic breading mix.
3. In large skillet, saute fish in butter, approximately 2 minutes on each side.
4. Serve with tarter sauce, lemon, or other condiments of choice.

Nutrition Information Per Serving

Calories 265	Fat 15 g	Fiber 3 g
Carbohydrates 7 g	Omega-3 Fats 4381 mg	Calcium 91 mg
Protein 25 g	Cholesterol 77 mg	Sodium 155 mg

Tuna Cakes
Preparation time: 15 minutes
Cooking time: 8 minutes
Yield: 4 servings

3 - 6 ounce cans tuna, drained
2 tablespoons Dijon mustard
2 teaspoons Old Bay seasoning
2 eggs
salt and pepper, to taste
1 cup basic flax breading (recipe, page 57)
1-2 tablespoons unsalted butter

1. Mix all ingredients, except the butter, together in medium bowl.
2. Make 8 tuna patties. If tuna patties fail to stick together, add a small amount of olive oil.
3. In large skillet, saute tuna cakes in butter, until lightly brown on both sides (about 4 minutes on each side).

Nutrition Information Per Serving

Calories 302	Fat 12 g	Fiber 3 g
Carbohydrates 8 g	Omega-3 Fats 2928 mg	Calcium 96 mg
Protein 39 g	Cholesterol 152 mg	Sodium 965 mg

Crab Cakes
Preparation time: 5 minutes
Cooking time: 10 minutes
Yield: 4 servings

2 – 7.5 ounce cans crabmeat, drained
2 tablespoons Dijon mustard
2 teaspoons Old Bay seasoning
2 eggs
salt and pepper, to taste
1 cup basic breading mix (recipe, page 57)
1-2 tablespoons unsalted butter

1. Mix all ingredients together, except butter, in a bowl.
2. Form mixture into 8 patties. If mixture fails to stick together, moisten with small amount of olive oil.
3. In large skillet, saute crab cakes in butter, until lightly brown on both sides (about 3-4 minutes for each side).
4. Serve with Dijon mustard or cocktail sauce.

Nutrition Information Per Serving

Calories 230	Fat 12 g	Fiber 3 g
Carbohydrates 8 g	Omega-3 Fats 2581 mg	Calcium 122 mg
Protein 23 g	Cholesterol 150 mg	Sodium 1257 mg

Crab Quiche
Preparation time: 15 minutes
Cooking time: 45-60 minutes

Yield: 8 servings

This recipe can easily be converted to a savory Chicken Quiche. Simply substitute 1 cup diced, cooked chicken for the crabmeat and add 1/4 teaspoon ground thyme for seasoning.

1 – 7.5 ounce can crab meat, drained or 5 ounces frozen crab
1 cup shredded swiss cheese
1/4 cup toasted flaxseed
1/3 cup minced onion
1 prepared frozen pie crust, deep dish
2 whole eggs
1 cup skim milk
1 tablespoon all-purpose flour
1-1/2 tablespoons water
salt, to taste
1/4 teaspoon pepper
Fresh chopped parsley, to garnish

1. Preheat oven to 425 F.
2. Combine crab, cheese, toasted flaxseed, and onion in medium bowl. Spread mixture in pie crust.
3. In medium bowl, beat eggs, then add skim milk and mix.
4. In separate small bowl, make slurry with flour and water, using fork.
5. Add slurry to egg mixture and blend in well; add salt and pepper and mix.
6. Pour egg mixture into pie crust.
7. Cook uncovered for 425 F for 15 minutes, reduce heat to 300 F and cook approximately 30 minutes. Garnish with parsley.

Nutrition Information Per Serving

Calories 221	Fat 13 g	Fiber 2 g
Carbohydrates 11 g	Omega-3 Fats 1522 mg	Calcium 220 mg
Protein 14 g	Cholesterol 91 mg	Sodium 264 mg

BEEF, PORK, and VEAL

Beef Burgundy
Preparation time: 20 minutes
Cooking time: 50 minutes
Yield: 4 servings

4 cubed beef steaks(4 ounces each)
seasoned flour (recipe, page 56)
1 tablespoon unsalted butter
2 tablespoons ground flaxseed
1 cup fresh mushrooms, sliced
1 – 15 ounce jar small whole onions, drained
1 clove garlic, chopped finely
1/8 teaspoon black pepper
1/2 cup burgundy
1 cup reduced sodium beef broth

1. Preheat oven to 350 F.
2. Dredge beef in seasoned flour, place in medium skillet, add butter, and cook till lightly brown.
3. Place in ungreased 8 X 8 square baking dish.
4. In medium bowl, add remaining ingredients, and mix together.
5. Pour ingredients over beef.
6. Cook covered in 350 F oven for 30-40 minutes, or until sauce is slightly thickened and beef is tender.
7. Serve with noodles or mashed potatoes.

Nutrition Information Per Serving

Calories 271	Fat 11 g	Fiber 2 g
Carbohydrates 5 g	Omega-3 Fats 1039 mg	Calcium 32 mg
Protein 32 g	Cholesterol 82 mg	Sodium 198 mg

Beef Stroganoff
Preparation time: 20 minutes
Cooking time: 40 minutes
Yield: 4 servings

1/4 cup all-purpose flour
salt, to taste
1/8 teaspoon black pepper
3 tablespoons ground flaxseed
1 pound beef sirloin, cut into strips
1-2 tablespoons unsalted butter
1 cup reduced sodium beef broth
1 tablespoon tomato paste
1 tablespoon Dijon mustard
1 tablespoon Worcestershire sauce
1 cup fresh mushrooms, sliced
1/4 cup dry sherry (optional)
3/4 cup lite sour cream

1. Mix flour, salt, pepper, and flaxseed together in bowl.
2. Coat beef with mixture.
3. In large saucepan, brown coated beef in butter.
4. Add in saucepan beef broth, tomato paste, mustard, Worcestershire sauce, and mushrooms.
5. Bring to boil, simmer covered for 30 minutes or until beef is tender.
6. Remove from heat. Fold in sherry and sour cream.
7. Serve over rice or noodles.

Nutrition Information Per Serving

Calories 293	Fat 14 g	Fiber 2 g
Carbohydrates 11 g	Omega-3 Fats 1481 mg	Calcium 85 mg
Protein 29 g	Cholesterol 92 mg	Sodium 336 mg

Swedish Meatballs
Preparation time: 15 minutes
Cooking time: 20 minutes
Yield: 6 servings

Meatballs
¼ cup minced onion
½ tablespoon extra virgin olive oil
8 ounces lean ground beef(chuck or sirloin)
8 ounces ground turkey
¼ cup ground flaxseed
2 whole eggs
salt, to taste
¼ teaspoon black pepper
¼ teaspoon ground nutmeg
¼ teaspoon ground allspice
¼ cup plain bread crumbs
½ cup water
1 tablespoon extra virgin olive oil

Sauce
1 -1 ounce package brown gravy mix, dry
¼ cup lite sour cream

1. In small saucepan, add olive oil and onions, cook over medium-high heat for about 2-3 minutes until tender. Set aside to cool.
2. Mix remaining meatball (except olive oil) ingredients together in large bowl, including onions. Form into meatballs, should have approximately 18 balls.
3. Brown meatballs in frying pan with olive oil until done, about 10-15 minutes, brown on all sides.
4. Make brown gravy according to package instructions. Take off heat, and fold in sour cream. Mix well together.
5. In same pan meatballs are in, pour over gravy/sour cream sauce Let simmer 2-3 minutes. Serve over egg noodles.

Nutrition Information Per Serving

Calories 241	Fat 15 g	Fiber 2 g
Carbohydrates 8 g	Omega-3 Fats 1368 mg	Calcium 58 mg
Protein 19 g	Cholesterol 129 mg	Sodium 389 mg

Stuffed Chili Peppers

Preparation time: 20 minutes
Cooking time: 60 minutes
Yield: 6 servings

8 ounces lean ground beef(chuck or sirloin)
8 ounces ground turkey
¼ cup ground flaxseed
2 whole eggs
salt, to taste
¼ teaspoon black pepper
¼ teaspoon ground nutmeg
¼ teaspoon ground allspice
¼ cup plain bread crumbs
½ cup water
6 medium sized green peppers, core removed
Uncle David's Marinara Sauce(recipe, page 84)
¼ cup parmesan cheese, shredded

1. Preheat oven to 350 F.
2. In large bowl, mix together beef, turkey, flax, eggs, salt, pepper, spices, bread crumbs, and water.
3 Fill peppers with equal portions of meat mixture.
4. Place in 9 X 13 baking dish(coated with non-stick spray).
5. Bake in 350 F oven for 30 minutes.
6.Drain liquid out, if needed. Pour marinara sauce over peppers. Bake for another 30 minutes.
7. Top with parmesan cheese.

Nutrition Information Per Serving

Calories 263	Fat 11 g	Fiber 5 g
Carbohydrates 20 g	Omega-3 Fats 1381 mg	Calcium 125 mg
Protein 22 g	Cholesterol 126 mg	Sodium 426 mg

Cabbage Rolls

Preparation time: 35 minutes
Cooking time: 60 minutes
Yield: 6 servings

18 cabbage leaves
1 pound ground turkey
1 small onion, chopped
3/4 cup ground flax
½ cup uncooked instant rice
1/2 cup reduced sodium beef broth
salt, to taste
1/8 teaspoon black pepper
1/8 teaspoon granulated garlic
1 – 15 ounce can tomato sauce

1. Preheat oven to 350 F.
2. In a large pan, pour boiling water over cabbage leaves.
3. Let sit for 10 minutes or until limp.
4. In large bowl, mix turkey, rice, onion, ground flax, seasonings, broth, and ½ cup tomato sauce together.
5. Divide mixture evenly between cabbage leaves and stuff each leaf. Place mixture on the bottom of the leaf. Fold the right side, roll up the leaf loosely. Tuck the left end into itself, closing the opening.
6. Prepare 8 X 8 baking dish with nonstick cooking spray, then place cabbage rolls seam side down in dish.
7. Cover with remaining tomato sauce and cover baking dish with plastic wrap first, then aluminum foil.
8. Cook for approximately 1 hour.

Nutrition Information Per Serving

Calories 268	Fat 13 g	Fiber 8 g
Carbohydrates 18 g	Omega-3 Fats 4014 mg	Calcium 109 mg
Protein 20 g	Cholesterol 60 mg	Sodium 561 mg

Horseradish Steak

Preparation time: 5 minutes
Cooking time: about 20 minutes
Yield: 4 servings

4 beef fillets(4-6 ounces each)
salt and pepper, as needed
horseradish flax crust (recipe, page 58)

1. Season fillet with salt and pepper.
2. Grill or broil beef fillet to desired doneness, approximately 16 minutes.
3. Top with horseradish flax crust.
4. Place under broiler or in hot oven (450 F) until topping is thoroughly heated; about 2 minutes.

Nutrition Information Per Serving

Calories 382	Fat 24 g	Fiber 4 g
Carbohydrates 13 g	Omega-3 Fats 2132 mg	Calcium 78 mg
Protein 28 g	Cholesterol 100 mg	Sodium 276 mg

Blackened Sirloin

Preparation time: 10 minutes
Cooking time: cook to preference
Yield: 4 servings

4 sirloin steaks(4-6 ounces each)

salt and pepper, to taste
1-2 tablespoons extra virgin olive oil
Cajun Flax Coating (recipe, page 59)

1. Season steak with salt and pepper.
2. Brush with olive oil.
3. Dredge in Cajun Flax Coating.
4. Cook in large skillet on high, making sure it is very hot before placing steaks in.
5. Cook till desired doneness.

Nutrition Information Per Serving

Calories 270	Fat 16 g	Fiber 4 g
Carbohydrates 4 g	Omega-3 Fats 2590 mg	Calcium 59 mg
Protein 27 g	Cholesterol 69 mg	Sodium 72 mg

Beef Fried Steak
Preparation time: 10 minutes
Cooking time: 10 minutes
Yield: 4 servings

4 beef cutlets(4 ounces each)
salt and pepper, to taste
seasoned flour (recipe, page 56)
egg wash (recipe, page 56)
basic flax breading (recipe, page 57)
1-2 tablespoons unsalted butter
1-2.75 ounce package peppered white sauce, prepared

1. Season beef cutlets with salt and pepper.
2. Dredge in flour, shake off excess.
3. Place in egg wash.
4. Coat with basic breading mix.
5. Place cutlets in large skillet, and cook with butter, 3-4 minutes on each side.

6. Serve with peppered white sauce.

Nutrition Information Per Serving

Calories 350	Fat 20 g	Fiber 4 g
Carbohydrates 13 g	Omega-3 Fats 2629 mg	Calcium 162 mg
Protein 29 g	Cholesterol 78 mg	Sodium 598 mg

Pork Cutlet with Pepper Sauce
Preparation time: 10 minutes
Cooking time: 10 minutes
Yield: 4 servings

4 pork cutlets(4-5 ounces each)
salt and pepper, to taste
seasoned flour (recipe, page 56)
egg wash (recipe, page 56)
basic flax breading (recipe, page 57)
1-2 tablespoons unsalted butter
1-2.75 ounce package peppered white sauce, prepared

1. Season pork cutlets with salt and pepper.
2. Dredge in flour, shake off excess.
3. Place in egg wash.
4. Coat with basic breading mix.
5. Saute in skillet with butter, 5-6 minutes on each side.
6. Serve with peppered white sauce.

Nutrition Information Per Serving

Calories 319	Fat 16 g	Fiber 4 g
Carbohydrates 13 g	Omega-3 Fats 2640 mg	Calcium 168 mg
Protein 29 g	Cholesterol 80 mg	Sodium 590 mg

Veal Piccata
Preparation time: 10 minutes
Cooking time: 8 minutes
Yield: 4 servings

8 slices veal leg (each slice about 2 oz)
seasoned flour (recipe, page 56)
egg wash (recipe, page 56)
basic breading recipe (recipe, page 57)
2-3 tablespoons extra virgin olive oil
2 fresh lemons, cut in half
1/4 cup white wine(optional)
1 tablespoon capers
fresh chopped parsley, to garnish

1. Slightly pound veal leg slices.
2. Dredge in seasoned flour.
3. Shake off excess flour.
4. Dip in egg wash.
5. Coat with basic breading mix.
6. In large skillet, cook and stir veal leg slices in olive oil
approximately 2 minutes on each side, and remove from pan.
7. Pour off excess olive oil in pan.
8. Deglaze the pan with juice from 2 fresh lemons.
9. Add the wine, stirring constantly until about half of the liquid is
gone.
10. Then add capers to liquid mixture for 1 to 2 minutes.
11. Pour liquid mixture over veal slices, garnish with parsley, and
serve.

Nutrition Information Per Serving

Calories 278	Fat 14 g	Fiber 4 g
Carbohydrates 9 g	Omega-3 Fats 2578 mg	Calcium 77 mg
Protein 28 g	Cholesterol 89 mg	Sodium 242 mg

POULTRY

Turkey Parmesan
Preparation time: 15 minutes
Cooking time: 20 minutes
Yield: 4 servings

4 slices raw turkey breast (4 ounces each)
seasoned flour (recipe, page 56)
egg wash (recipe, page 56)
basic breading mix (recipe, page 57)
1-2 tablespoons extra virgin olive oil
1 cup seasoned tomato sauce or prepared spaghetti sauce
4 slices part skim mozzarella cheese (1 ounce each)
1 ounce fresh Parmesan cheese, shredded

1. Preheat oven to 350 F .
2. Slightly pound turkey breast.
3. Dredge in seasoned flour and shake off excess.
4. Dip in egg wash.
5. Coat with basic breading mix.
6. In large skillet, saute turkey breast in olive oil, approximately 4 minutes on each side, and remove from pan, place in baking sheet (sprayed with non-stick spray).
7. Top cutlets with tomato or spaghetti sauce.
8. Finish with 1 slice mozzarella cheese and top with Parmesan cheese.
9. Place in 350 F oven, until bubbly or cheese melted, approximately 10-15 minutes.

Nutrition Information Per Serving

Calories 345	Fat 15 g	Fiber 4 g
Carbohydrates 12 g	Omega-3 Fats 2613 mg	Calcium 297 mg
Protein 40 g	Cholesterol 89 mg	Sodium 698 mg

Pecan Crusted Duck Breast
Preparation time: 12 minutes
Cooking time: 10 minutes
Yield: 4 servings

4 skinless, boneless duck breasts (4 ounces each)
seasoned flour (recipe, page 56)
egg wash (recipe, page 56)
pecan flax breading (recipe, page 57)
1-2 tablespoons extra virgin olive oil
1 – 8.5 ounce jar plum sauce

1. Slightly pound duck breasts.
2. Dredge in seasoned flour and shake off excess.
3. Dip in egg wash.
4. Coat with pecan flax breading.
5. In large skillet, cook duck breasts in olive oil using medium-low heat, approximately 4 minutes on each side. For well-done duck, bake 10 minutes in 350 F oven, instead.
6. Remove from pan. Cut duck breasts diagonally(8-10 slices), put on plate, and drizzle with hot plum sauce.

Nutrition Information Per Serving

Calories 394	Fat 17 g	Fiber 4 g
Carbohydrates 32 g	Omega-3 Fats 2706 mg	Calcium 65 mg
Protein 27 g	Cholesterol 87 mg	Sodium 452 mg

Cajun Chicken
Preparation time: 5 minutes
Cooking time: 10 minutes
Yield: 4 servings

4 chicken breasts, skinless, boneless (4 ounces each)
seasoned flour (recipe, page 56)
egg wash (recipe, page 56)

Cajun flax breading (recipe, page 59)
1-2 tablespoons extra virgin olive oil
1 cup creole sauce

1. Slightly pound chicken breasts.
2. Dredge in seasoned flour and shake off excess.
3. Dip in egg wash.
4. Coat with Cajun flax breading.
5. In medium skillet, saute chicken in olive oil approximately 3-4 minutes on each side, and remove from pan.
6. Top with warm creole sauce.

Nutrition Information Per Serving

Calories 369	Fat 14 g	Fiber 11 g
Carbohydrates 25 g	Omega-3 Fats 3973 mg	Calcium 338 mg
Protein 36 g	Cholesterol 66 mg	Sodium 608 mg

Walnut Duck Breast
Preparation time: 12 minutes
Cooking time: 10 minutes
Yield: 4 servings

4 boneless, skinless duck breasts (4 ounces each)
seasoned flour (recipe, page 56)
egg wash (recipe, page 56)
walnut breading mix (recipe, page 57)
1-2 tablespoons extra virgin olive oil

Cranberry Orange Relish
1 cup fresh cranberries
2 oranges, each cut into six wedges, remove seeds(1 peeled)
1/4 cup white sugar
½ cup pecans, toasted

1. Cut each orange into 6 wedges and remove seeds. Peel one of the oranges, but leave skin on the other.
2. Combine oranges with all other relish ingredients and place in food processor or blender. Blend until roughly chopped.
3. Add sugar to taste.
4. Chill until needed.

Preparation of duck breasts
1. Slightly pound duck breasts.
2. Dredge in seasoned flour and shake off excess.
3. Dip in egg wash.
4. Coat with walnut flax breading mix.
5. In skillet, saute duck in olive oil approximately 3-4 minutes on each side, and remove from pan.
6. Serve with chilled cranberry orange relish.

Nutrition Information Per Serving

Calories 422	Fat 22 g	Fiber 7 g
Carbohydrates 30 g	Omega-3 Fats 3164 mg	Calcium 86 mg
Protein 28 g	Cholesterol 87 mg	Sodium 147 mg

Almond Chicken
Preparation time: 5 minutes
Cooking time: 10 minutes
Yield: 4 servings

4 chicken breasts, boneless, skinless (4 ounces each)
seasoned flour (recipe, page 56)
egg wash (recipe, page 56)
almond flax breading (recipe, page 58)
1-2 tablespoons extra virgin olive oil

1. Slightly pound chicken breasts.
2. Dredge in seasoned flour and shake off excess.
3. Dip in egg wash.

4. Coat with Almond flax breading.

5. In skillet, saute chicken in olive oil approximately 3-4 minutes on each side, and remove from pan.

Nutrition Information Per Serving

Calories 268	Fat 12 g	Fiber 4 g
Carbohydrates 9 g	Omega-3 Fats 2583 mg	Calcium 74 mg
Protein 30 g	Cholesterol 66 mg	Sodium 156 mg

Chicken Crepes
Preparation time: 15 minutes
Cooking time: 20 minutes
Yield: 6 servings

1 pound cooked chicken, skinless, boneless, diced
3 cups reduced sodium chicken broth
1 large onion, chopped
2 stalks celery, cut in 1-inch pieces
1 bay leaf
1/4 teaspoon black pepper
1/4 cup all purpose flour
1/2 cup cold water
1/2 cup lite sour cream
1/4 cup dry sherry (optional)
12 flax crepes
chopped fresh parsley (for garnish)

Flax Crepes
4 eggs
1 ½ cups skim milk
2 tablespoons unsalted butter, melted
1 cup all-purpose flour
salt, to taste
1/4 cup toasted flaxseed

To Prepare Crepes
1. In mixing bowl, beat eggs.
2. Add remaining ingredients and mix together.
3. Pour ¼ cup mixture on small round hot pan. Tilt pan and rotate clockwise to coat evenly bottom of pan. As edges start to slightly crisp use a spatula to gently flip over.
4. When lightly brown, turn over and repeat.

To Prepare Chicken
1. In large sauce pan, place chicken, broth, onion, celery, bay leaf, and pepper.
2. Bring to simmer.
3. In small cup, make a slurry using water and flour, using a fork
4. Stir into broth. Heat mixture until boils and thickens, stirring constantly.
5. Add sherry and sour cream into mixture.
6. Fill crepes with mixture and roll.

For family-style service, serve the crepes and topping separately (feel free to stack the crepes on a platter) and let everybody build their own.

Nutrition Information Per Serving

Calories 393	Fat 15 g	Fiber 4 g
Carbohydrates 27 g	Omega-3 Fats 1861 mg	Calcium 153 mg
Protein 36 g	Cholesterol 222 mg	Sodium 609 mg

Southwestern Turkey Fillet
Preparation time: 20 minutes
Cooking time: 20 minutes
Yield: 4 servings

4 slices raw turkey breast, skinless, boneless (4 ounces each)
seasoned flour (recipe, page 56)
egg wash (recipe, page 56)

southwestern flax breading (recipe, page 57)
1-2 tablespoons extra virgin olive oil
1 cup salsa
4 ounces low-fat cheddar cheese, grated

1. Preheat oven to 400 F.
2. Slightly pound turkey breast.
3. Dredge in seasoned flour and shake off any excess.
4. Dip in egg wash.
5. Coat with southwestern flax breading.
6. In large skillet, saute in olive oil, approximately 3-4 minutes on each side, and remove from pan; put in baking sheet (coated with non-stick spray).
7. Top with warm chunky, spicy salsa and grated cheddar cheese.
8. Place in 400 F oven, uncovered, until cheese is melted and meat is thoroughly cooked, about 15 minutes.

Nutrition Information Per Serving

Calories 317	Fat 12 g	Fiber 5 g
Carbohydrates 14 g	Omega-3 Fats 2594 mg	Calcium 223 mg
Protein 39 g	Cholesterol 76 mg	Sodium 499 mg

Oven Baked Fried Chicken
Preparation time: 5 minutes
Cooking time: 25 minutes
Yield: 4 servings

Everybody loves fried chicken, but you can improve the health-value by skipping the fat in frying and using your oven instead. For this recipe, we've used the basic flax breading recipe, but feel free to try any of the other breadings given in Chapter 3, if you're feeling adventurous.

4 boneless, skinless chicken breasts (4 ounces each)
egg wash (recipe, page 56)
basic flax breading (recipe, page 57)

1. Preheat oven to 375 F.
2. Dip chicken breasts in egg wash.
3. Completely coat with basic breading mixture.
4. Place on ungreased baking sheet uncovered and cook at 375 F for approximately 25 minutes.

Nutrition Information Per Serving

Calories 277	Fat 9 g	Fiber 3 g
Carbohydrates 7 g	Omega-3 Fats 2522 mg	Calcium 86 mg
Protein 39 g	Cholesterol 97 mg	Sodium 451 mg

June's Chicken Stir Fry
Preparation time: 10 minutes
Cooking time: 20 minutes
Yield: 4 servings

This recipe is from June and Roy Swanson of Dewitt, Iowa. They started incorporating flaxseed in 1999, due to Roy's high blood lipid levels, as well as a high prostate count. Since they changed to a more healthier way of eating, which includes flax, Roy's blood lipid levels and prostate count continue to be normal.

1 ½ cups low sodium chicken broth
3 tablespoons low sodium soy sauce or Tamari sauce
2 ½ tablespoons cornstarch
1 tablespoon brown sugar
1 teaspoon garlic powder
1 teaspoon ground ginger
¼ teaspoon crushed red pepper(adjust to taste)
¼ cup ground flaxseed
1-2 tablespoons extra virgin olive oil
1 pound boneless, skinless chicken breasts(cut in strips)
4 cups frozen Chinese vegetable mix

1. In saucepan, mix broth, soy sauce, cornstarch, sugar, garlic powder, ginger, and red pepper. Bring to boil, boil for 1 minute. Remove from heat and stir in ground flaxseed.

2. Stir fry chicken in large skillet or wok with olive oil, until browned. Add vegetables and stir fry until crisp and tender.
3. Add sauce mixture and serve with rice.

Nutrition Information Per Serving

Calories 292	Fat 10 g	Fiber 5 g
Carbohydrates 19 g	Omega-3 Fats 1996 mg	Calcium 54 mg
Protein 32 g	Cholesterol 72 mg	Sodium 512 mg

Vegetarian Style

June's Tofu Stir Fry
Preparation time: 10 minutes
Cooking time: 20 minutes
Yield: 4 servings

Here is a vegetarian alternative from June and Roy Swanson

1 ½ cups low sodium chicken broth
3 tablespoons low sodium soy sauce or Tamari sauce
2 ½ tablespoons cornstarch
1 tablespoon brown sugar
1 teaspoon garlic powder
1 teaspoon ground ginger
¼ teaspoon crushed red pepper(adjust to taste)
¼ cup ground flaxseed
1-2 tablespoons extra virgin olive oil
1 pound marinated/baked tofu(below)
4 cups frozen Chinese vegetable mix

Marinated/baked tofu
¼ cup water
¼ cup low sodium soy sauce or Tamari sauce
2 tablespoons cooking sherry wine
1 tablespoon honey

2 cloves garlic, minced
1 tablespoon vinegar
1 – 12 ounce box extra firm tofu, cut into ½" cubes

1. In bowl, mix together water, soy sauce, wine, honey, garlic, and vinegar.
2. Place tofu cubes in shallow dish and pour mixture over cubes.
3. Cover dish with plastic wrap and place in refrigerator for 2 days. Turn at least 1-2 times each day.
4. After 2 days, transfer cubes to a clean container & freeze for 2 days.
5. When ready to use, take out and thaw before cooking. Cubes will last in freezer for about 2 months.

*Note: Don't have the time to make baked tofu? Look for baked tofu (already seasoned) in your local health food store or supermarket!

To Prepare Stir Fry

1. In saucepan, mix broth, soy sauce, cornstarch, sugar, garlic powder, ginger, and red pepper. Bring to boil, boil for 1 minute. Remove from heat and stir in ground flaxseed.
2. Stir fry tofu in large skillet or wok with olive oil, until browned. Add vegetables and stir fry until crisp and tender.
3. Add sauce mixture and serve with rice.

Nutrition Information Per Serving

Calories 204	Fat 8 g	Fiber 5 g
Carbohydrates 24 g	Omega-3 Fats 1996 mg	Calcium 82 mg
Protein 12 g	Cholesterol 0 mg	Sodium 340 mg

Pan Fried Greek Cheese (Kasseri)
Preparation time: 5 minutes
Cooking time: 5 minutes
Yield: 4 servings

4 slices (2 ounces each) Kasseri cheese
1 tablespoon extra virgin olive oil
¼ cup ground flaxseed
¼ cup all-purpose flour
1 ounce Brandy
1 fresh lemon

1. Brush cheese with olive oil.
2. Mix flaxseed and flour in medium mixing bowl.
3. Dredge cheese in flax-flour mixture.
4. Place in hot cast iron skillet and cook on stovetop for 1 minute on high heat.
5. Turn over cheese, flambee with brandy (watch out for flame).
6. Squeeze juice from lemon over cheese to douse the flame.

Nutrition Information Per Serving

Calories 266	Fat 19 g	Fiber 3 g
Carbohydrates 8 g	Omega-3 Fats 1952 mg	Calcium 101 mg
Protein 13 g	Cholesterol 26 mg	Sodium 212 mg

Fried Green Tomatoes w/ Marinara Sauce
Preparation time: 10 minutes
Cooking time: 10 minutes
Yield: 2 servings

2 green tomatoes, sliced 1/4 inch thick
salt and pepper, to taste
seasoned flour (recipe, page 56)
egg wash (recipe, page 56)
basic flax breading (recipe, page 57)
1-2 tablespoons extra virgin olive oil
Uncle Dave's Marinara Sauce, heated (recipe, page 84)
Fresh shredded Parmesan cheese, for garnish
Fresh basil, chopped, for garnish

1. Season tomatoes with salt and pepper.
2. Dredge in seasoned flour.
3. Dip in egg wash.
4. Then into basic flax breading.
5. In medium skillet, saute in olive oil till golden brown on each side.
6. Remove from pan.
7. Put heated marinara sauce on each plate, top with tomatoes.
8. Sprinkle with fresh Parmesan cheese and fresh basil.

Nutrition Information Per Serving

Calories 297	Fat 19 g	Fiber 8 g
Carbohydrates 23 g	Omega-3 Fats 5088 mg	Calcium 172 mg
Protein 10 g	Cholesterol 2 mg	Sodium 413 mg

Vegetable Stew
Preparation time: 15 minutes
Cooking time: 1 hour 15 minutes
Yield: 6 servings

2 tablespoons extra virgin olive oil
1/2 medium onion, chopped
1 cup sliced celery
3 cloves garlic, minced
1 cup red wine(optional)
2 cups reduced sodium chicken broth
2 bay leaves
1 teaspoon thyme
2 cups V-8 juice
1 – 14.5 ounce can diced tomatoes
1-1/2 pounds red potatoes (washed, but not peeled), cut into 1-inch cubes
1 pound baby carrots
1 cup peas, frozen
¼ cup ground flaxseed
1/4 cup chopped fresh parsley

1. Preheat oven to 350 F.
2. Place olive oil in dutch oven or large roasting pan over medium-high heat, add onion and celery, and cook until tender about 5 minutes. Add garlic, cook 1 minute.
3. Add remaining ingredients, except for peas, flax, and parsley.
4. Place in 350 F with lid, cook for 45 minutes - 1 hour, or until potatoes are tender.
5. Remove from oven, fold in flax and peas, let stand 5 minutes. Remove bay leaves. Fold in chopped parsley and serve.

Nutrition Information Per Serving

Calories 264	Fat 8 g	Fiber 7 g
Carbohydrates 43 g	Omega-3 Fats 1363 mg	Calcium 96 mg
Protein 8 g	Cholesterol 0 mg	Sodium 652 mg

Eggplant Parmesan
Preparation time: 15 minutes
Cooking time: 20 minutes
Yield: 6 servings

2 whole eggs
3 tablespoons water
salt, to taste
all purpose flour
1 large eggplant, cut into ½ inch slices
1 cup ground flaxseed
1-1/2 cups plain bread crumbs
1-2 tablespoons extra virgin olive oil
1/3 cup grated Parmesan cheese
1/8 teaspoon red pepper flakes
4 ounces sliced Monterey Jack cheese
¾ cup tomato sauce

2 tablespoons fresh oregano leaves or 2 teaspoons dried

1. Preheat oven to 400 F.
2. Beat in a shallow bowl eggs, water and salt.
3. Sprinkle flour onto paper towel—just enough to coat both sides of eggplant slices.
4. Mix ground flaxseed and bread crumbs together in separate bowl.
5. Dip flour coated eggplant in egg mixture, followed by bread crumb/flax mixture. Repeat with all eggplant slices.
6. Heat olive oil over medium heat, add eggplant slices, and brown both sides.
7. Place on nonstick cooking sheet.
8. Mix together Parmesan cheese and red pepper flakes. Top eggplant slices with sliced cheese, tomato sauce, sprinkling of oregano, and Parmesan cheese mixture.
9. Bake at 400 F for 8-10 minutes until bubbly–serve immediately.

Nutrition Information Per Serving

Calories 350	Fat 19 g	Fiber 9 g
Carbohydrates 28 g	Omega-3 Fats 5195 mg	Calcium 287 mg
Protein 17 g	Cholesterol 84 mg	Sodium 586 mg

Pizza, Pizza, Pizza 10

How can we leave our tour of Italy behind without reference to it's most beloved export? You guessed it, I'm talking about pizza! Whether you roll and toss it like the pros or use the convenience of a bread-making machine, you can create a delicious flax-based pizza crust!

Homemade Flaxseed Pizza Dough
Preparation time: 1 hour 30 minutes
Yield: 2 - 12" pizzas (16 slices)

You'll find that making your own pizza crust from scratch is lots easier than you'd expect. And there's something really satisfying about kneading fresh-made dough. You might never go back to store-bought again!

1 package (2-1/4 teaspoons) active dry yeast
1-3/4 cups warm water (between 105 and 115 F)
2-3/4 cups all purpose flour
1 cup ground flaxseed
1/2 cup whole wheat flour
2 tablespoons extra virgin olive oil
½ teaspoon salt
1 tablespoon white sugar
1/4 cup Parmesan cheese, grated

1. Add water to yeast in small bowl, let sit for 5 minutes.
2. Mix remaining ingredients together in medium bowl. Add water/yeast mixture and combine thoroughly.
3. Knead for 10 minutes on a lightly floured surface, until dough is smooth and slightly elastic.

4. Place dough back in bowl, cover with plastic, and let rise in warm area, about 1 hour, until dough doubles in volume.
5. Spray two 12-inch pans with non-stick cooking spray.
6. Punch dough down, and divide in half; roll each half in a ball, cover in plastic, put in large bowl, and let rest for 10-15 minutes.
7. Remove plastic and flatten each ball into a 12-inch-diameter circle on a slightly floured surface.
8. Place dough on baking sheets.
9. Brush crust lightly with olive oil; dock the dough with fork or pizza docker (punching holes all over crust to prevent bubbling).
10. Pre-bake in 400 F oven for 6-8 minutes will result in a crunchier crust. Now these crusts may be frozen for use at a later time. (optional)

Nutrition Information Per Slice

Calories 153	Fat 6 g	Fiber 3 g
Carbohydrates 20 g	Omega-3 Fats 1950 mg	Calcium 41 mg
Protein 5 g	Cholesterol 1 mg	Sodium 100 mg

Pizza Crust for the Bread Machine
Preparation time: 1 hour 30 minutes
Yield: 2 – 12" pizzas (16 slices)

If you've opted for the convenience of a bread-making machine, you can press it into service to make your pizza dough. Here's how:

1-1/4 teaspoons active dry yeast (or 1 teaspoon quick rising yeast)
1-3/4 cups warm water (between 105 and 115 F)
2 cups bread flour
1 cup ground flaxseed
1/2 cup whole wheat flour
2 tablespoons extra virgin olive oil
½ teaspoon salt

1. Assemble according to bread machine directions and put on dough cycle.
2. Spray baking sheets with non-stick cooking spray.
3. Take dough out of bread machine and place it on a slightly floured surface. Flatten the dough to form a 12-inch-diameter circle.
4. Place dough on baking sheet.
5. Pre-bake in 400 F oven for 6-8 minutes will result in a crunchier crust. Now these crusts may be frozen for use at a later time. (optional)

Nutrition Information Per Slice

Calories 127	Fat 5 g	Fiber 3 g
Carbohydrates 15 g	Omega-3 Fats 1949 mg	Calcium 23 mg
Protein 4 g	Cholesterol 0 mg	Sodium 76 mg

Now that you've got a basic pizza crust, you've got a wealth of options for toppings. Each topping recipe is for one 12" pizza divided into 8 slices. In the suggestions that follow, you'll sometimes find specific directions for "dressing" your pizza, but there are a few general guidelines to keep in mind no matter which topping you choose:

- Spread sauce evenly over the crust, but avoid getting any liquid ingredients on the outer edges, where it's likely to burn.
- Evenly distribute toppings on sauce.
- Finish with layer of appropriate cheese.
- Bake fully topped pizza at 400 F according to cooking time, or until cheese is lightly brown and crust is crisp.

The Toppings

Traditional Italian Style
Preparation time: 20 minutes
Cooking time: 12-15 minutes

1 – 8 ounce can pizza sauce
6 ounces Italian sausage, cooked
4 ounces part-skim mozzarella cheese, shredded

Nutrition Information Per Slice

Calories 250	Fat 14 g	Fiber 3 g
Carbohydrates 18 g	Omega-3 Fats 2063 mg	Calcium 138 mg
Protein 13 g	Cholesterol 24 mg	Sodium 503 mg

Basil & Tomato
Preparation time: 20 minutes
Cooking time: 12-15 minutes

1 tablespoon fresh chopped garlic
1-2 tablespoons extra virgin olive oil
4-6 ounces part skim mozzarella cheese
2 roma tomatoes, cut in 1/4 inch slices
2 tablespoons chiffonade of basil(thinly sliced)

Brush pizza dough with olive oil and garlic. Top with cheese. Arrange tomatoes on top of cheese. Finish with fresh basil and bake.

Nutrition Information Per Slice

Calories 186	Fat 10 g	Fiber 3 g
Carbohydrates 17 g	Omega-3 Fats 1981 mg	Calcium 130 mg
Protein 8 g	Cholesterol 8 mg	Sodium 153 mg

Bacon, Lettuce, Tomato
Preparation time: 15 minutes
Cooking time: 20 minutes

2-4 tablespoons low fat mayonnaise
4-6 ounces part skim mozzarella cheese, shredded
1/3 cup bacon, cooked, diced
2 roma tomatoes, sliced into 1/4 inch thick slices
1 cup shredded lettuce
1 roma tomato, diced, seeds and juice removed

Brush crust with mayonnaise. Top with cheese, add bacon, next tomatoes. Bake in oven until done. Top with lettuce and diced tomatoes.

Nutrition Information Per Slice

Calories 203	Fat 11 g	Fiber 3 g
Carbohydrates 17 g	Omega-3 Fats 1971 mg	Calcium 128 mg
Protein 9 g	Cholesterol 11 mg	Sodium 233 mg

Four Cheese
Preparation time: 15 minutes
Cooking time: 20 minutes

1-2 tablespoons extra virgin olive oil
2 roma tomatoes, thinly sliced
2 ounces part skim mozzarella cheese
2 ounces romano cheese
2 ounces havarti cheese
2 ounces fontina cheese
¼ cup fresh basil, thinly sliced

Nutrition Information Per Slice

Calories 248	Fat 15 g	Fiber 3 g
Carbohydrates 17 g	Omega-3 Fats 2048 mg	Calcium 238 mg
Protein 12 g	Cholesterol 26 mg	Sodium 297 mg

Vegetarian
Preparation time: 15 minutes
Cooking time: 20 minutes

1 teaspoon extra virgin olive oil
1/4 cup sauteed zucchini strips
1/4 cup sauteed red and yellow pepper strips
1/4 cup sauteed eggplant strips
1/4 cup sauteed sliced mushrooms
¾ cup pizza sauce
6 ounces part skim mozzarella cheese, shredded
salt and pepper to taste

In large pan, sauté vegetables in olive oil. Spread pizza sauce, top with vegetables and mozzarella cheese. After baking, add salt and pepper to taste.

Nutrition Information Per Slice

Calories 185	Fat 9 g	Fiber 3 g
Carbohydrates 18 g	Omega-3 Fats 1975 mg	Calcium 133 mg
Protein 9 g	Cholesterol 8 mg	Sodium 268 mg

Californian Style
Preparation time: 20 minutes
Cooking time: 20 minutes

¾ cup seasoned tomato sauce
1/3 cup eggplant, diced
1/4 cup sliced mushrooms
1/4 cup red onion, diced
1/3 cup broccoli, chopped
2-4 tablespoons black olives, drained and sliced
6 ounces shredded mozzarella cheese
2 tablespoons thinly sliced basil

Nutrition Information Per Slice

Calories 203	Fat 10 g	Fiber 4 g
Carbohydrates 19 g	Omega-3 Fats 1986 mg	Calcium 188 mg
Protein 11 g	Cholesterol 12 mg	Sodium 353 mg

Chicken Pesto

Preparation time: 15 minutes
Cooking time: 15 minutes

1-2 teaspoons extra virgin olive oil
3 tablespoons prepared pesto sauce (recipe, page 86)
6 ounces diced grilled chicken
6 ounces part skim mozzarella cheese, shredded
1/4 cup fresh Parmesan cheese, shredded

Nutrition Information Per Slice

Calories 227	Fat 11 g	Fiber 4 g
Carbohydrates 16 g	Omega-3 Fats 2457 mg	Calcium 154 mg
Protein 16 g	Cholesterol 27 mg	Sodium 243 mg

Southwestern

Preparation time: 20 minutes
Cooking time: 20 minutes

¼ cup green pepper, sliced
¼ cup onion, sliced
½ cup tomatoes, diced
6 ounces grilled marinated chicken, diced
8 ounces reduced fat cheddar cheese, shredded
sour cream to taste
Fajita seasoning to taste

After baking, add sour cream and fajita seasoning to taste.

Nutrition Information Per Slice

Calories 216	Fat 8 g	Fiber 4 g
Carbohydrates 17 g	Omega-3 Fats 1969 mg	Calcium 146 mg
Protein 18 g	Cholesterol 24 mg	Sodium 316 mg

Pepperoni Mushroom
Preparation time: 15 minutes
Cooking time: 15-20 minutes

¾ cup pizza sauce
1/3 cup sliced pepperoni
3/4 cup sliced mushrooms
3 ounces part skim mozzarella cheese, shredded
3 ounces reduced fat cheddar cheese, shredded

Nutrition Information Per Slice

Calories 209	Fat 10 g	Fiber 3 g
Carbohydrates 18 g	Omega-3 Fats 1971 mg	Calcium 151 mg
Protein 11 g	Cholesterol 11 mg	Sodium 407 mg

Oriental
Preparation time: 15 minutes
Cooking time: 15-20 minutes

½ cup peanut sauce
1/4 cup scallions, thinly sliced
6 ounces cooked diced chicken
½ cup rice noodles, cooked
6 ounces part skim mozzarella cheese, shredded.

Nutrition Information Per Slice

Calories 253	Fat 12 g	Fiber 4 g
Carbohydrates 19 g	Omega-3 Fats 1970 mg	Calcium 136 mg
Protein 17 g	Cholesterol 26 mg	Sodium 255 mg

Alfredo Chicken
Preparation time: 15 minutes
Cooking time: 15-20 minutes

¾ cup alfredo sauce (recipe, page 85)
6 ounces cooked diced chicken
6 ounces part skim mozzarella cheese, shredded
2 tablespoons fresh Parmesan cheese, shredded

Nutrition Information Per Slice

Calories 239	Fat 11 g	Fiber 3 g
Carbohydrates 17 g	Omega-3 Fats 2108 mg	Calcium 218 mg
Protein 18 g	Cholesterol 32 mg	Sodium 310 mg

Taco
Preparation time: 15 minutes
Cooking time: 15-20 minutes

½ cup taco sauce
6 ounces Mexican Flaxmeat (recipe, page 187)
6 ounces colby cheese, shredded
½ cup diced tomatoes
1 cup shredded lettuce
1/2 cup tortilla chips, crumbled
sour cream and salsa, to taste

Add lettuce, chips, sour cream, and salsa after done baking.

Nutrition Information Per Slice

Calories 280	Fat 16 g	Fiber 4 g
Carbohydrates 20 g	Omega-3 Fats 2778 mg	Calcium 194 mg
Protein 14 g	Cholesterol 37 mg	Sodium 356 mg

Artichoke & Spinach
Preparation time: 15 minutes
Cooking time: 15-20 minutes

¾ cup chopped artichoke hearts
1/4 cup low-fat mayonnaise
1/4 cup Parmesan cheese, grated
1/2 cup chopped cooked spinach
4 ounces part skim mozzarella cheese, shredded
6 ounces cooked diced chicken

In a separate bowl, place artichoke, mayonnaise, Parmesan cheese, spinach, and mozzarella cheese and mix well. Spread on pizza crust, top with chicken and bake.

Nutrition Information Per Slice

Calories 250	Fat 12 g	Fiber 4 g
Carbohydrates 19 g	Omega-3 Fats 1988 mg	Calcium 182 mg
Protein 17 g	Cholesterol 28 mg	Sodium 324 mg

Hola Mexico

South of the border treats fill the shelves of grocery stores. Now you to can enjoy these tasty treats at home with a flax twist.

Mexican Flax Meat
Preparation time: 5 minutes
Cooking time: 10 minutes

1 pound ground turkey
½ medium onion, chopped
salt, to taste
½ teaspoon black pepper
½ teaspoon cumin
½ teaspoon chili powder
½ teaspoon granulated garlic or ¼ teaspoon garlic powder
½ cup ground flaxseed

1. Brown turkey in skillet, and add onion and spices. Cook for 5 minutes.
2. Take pan off heat and mix in ground flax.

Nutrition Information Per 3 Ounce Serving

Calories 188	Fat 12 g	Fiber 4 g
Carbohydrates 1 g	Omega-3 Fats 2993 mg	Calcium 45 mg
Protein 18 g	Cholesterol 67 mg	Sodium 87 mg

Mexican Lasagna

Preparation time: 15 minutes
Cooking time: 35-45 minutes
Yield: 6 servings

1 – 16 ounce can Fat Free Refried Beans
1 – 10 ounce can Enchilada sauce
9 – 6 inch corn tortilla
Mexican Flax Meat
½ cup Monterey Jack cheese, shredded
½ cup reduced fat cheddar cheese, shredded
1 – 4 ounce can diced green chilies

1. Preheat oven to 350 F.
2. Place refried beans and 5 ounces Enchilada sauce in medium sized mixing bowl. Blend well.
3. In 9 X 13 pan (coated with non-stick spray), assemble as follows: ½ refried bean mixture, 3 corn tortillas, all Mexican Flax Meat, 3 corn tortillas, other ½ refried bean mixture, top with diced chilies, top with remaining 3 tortillas, rest of Enchilada sauce, lastly shredded cheeses.
4. Bake in 350 F oven for 35-45 minutes.
5. Let sit for about 10 minutes before cutting and serving.

Nutrition Information Per Serving

Calories 356	Fat 14 g	Fiber 8 g
Carbohydrates 29 g	Omega-3 Fats 2665 mg	Calcium 207 mg
Protein 26 g	Cholesterol 68 mg	Sodium 807 mg

Enchilada

Preparation time: 10 minutes
Cooking time: 30-40 minutes
Yield: 6 servings

12 corn tortillas

Mexican Flax Meat
1 – 10 ounce can Enchilada sauce
½ cup Monterey Jack cheese, shredded
½ cup reduced fat cheddar cheese, shredded
lite sour cream, as desired

1. Preheat oven to 350 F.
2. Fill corn tortillas with Mexican Flax Meat, roll tortillas, and place in 9 X 13 pan (coated with non-stick spray).
3. Pour over Enchilada sauce, top with cheeses.
4. Bake in 350 F oven for about 30-40 minutes.
5. Top with sour cream if desired.

Nutrition Information Per Serving

Calories 314	Fat 15 g	Fiber 5 g
Carbohydrates 21 g	Omega-3 Fats 2665 mg	Calcium 220 mg
Protein 23 g	Cholesterol 68 mg	Sodium 386 mg

Tacos
Preparation time: 10 minutes
Yield: 6 servings

12 taco shells, hard
Mexican Flax Meat
½ cup reduced fat cheddar cheese, shredded
1 cup shredded lettuce
tomato,diced

1. Stuff taco shells with Mexican Flax Meat, cheese, lettuce, and tomato.
2. Add condiments as desired (like lite sour cream).

Nutrition Information Per Serving

Calories 313	Fat 18 g	Fiber 6 g
Carbohydrates 19 g	Omega-3 Fats 2814 mg	Calcium 125 mg
Protein 20 g	Cholesterol 62 mg	Sodium 236 mg

Burrito Wraps
Preparation time: 10 minutes
Yield: 6 servings

1 – 16 ounce can Fat Free Refried Beans
6 – 12 inch flour tortilla
Mexican Flax Meat
1 cup shredded lettuce
½ cup reduced fat cheddar cheese, shredded
1 tomato, diced

1. Heat refried beans till hot.
2. Lay out flour tortilla, in center place Mexican Flax Meat, lettuce, cheese, refried beans, and tomato in equal portions.
3. Fold sides to center, fold bottom up, and roll.
4. Cut diagonal. Serve w/ salsa and sour cream if desired.

Nutrition Information Per Serving

Calories 477	Fat 17 g	Fiber 10 g
Carbohydrates 52 g	Omega-3 Fats 2710 mg	Calcium 170 mg
Protein 28 g	Cholesterol 62 mg	Sodium 826 mg

Smooth as Silk 12

Smoothies are very popular these days, and no wonder! They're convenient, nutritious, and perfectly suited to today's on-the-go lifestyles. A good smoothie can even stand in for a light meal. And kids love smoothies, never realizing that they're getting good, solid nutrition in that creamy drink. So if you're worried that your children may not be getting enough of their necessary nutrients—or if you're concerned that your *own* diet may be missing a few vital elements—smoothies are a tasty way to make up the difference. All you need is a blender or food processor, and you can create an infinite variety of great-tasting smoothies right at home! Of course, to make your smoothies even *more* nutritious, we recommend you add flax. But no matter what ingredients you use, you'll get the best results if you keep in mind these 4 basic steps:

> Start with a 1/2 to 1 cup liquid base
> Add fruit
> Add flavorings
> Add ground flax and/or flax oil last

For many smoothies, the liquid base is often milk—cow, soy, or rice. You add the flax last because you want it to be absolutely fresh when you drink it. We've had fun in our test kitchen, inventing the following recipes and "tweaking" them for the best flavor. And once you get into the smoothie habit, we're sure you'll be concocting your own exotic versions of this nutritious beverage choice. Until then, try out some of our favorites!

Banana Berry Supreme
Yield: 2 cups

1 cup skim milk
1 frozen banana, sliced
1/2 cup frozen mixed berries (raspberries, blueberries, and
blackberries)
2 tablespoons ground flaxseed

Nutrition Information

Calories 290	Fat 8 g	Fiber 9 g
Carbohydrates 45 g	Omega-3 Fats 3926 mg	Calcium 351 mg
Protein 13 g	Cholesterol 5 mg	Sodium 135 mg

Raspberry Cream
Yield: 2 cups

1 cup skim milk
1/6(about 2 ounces) block silken tofu
1/2 cup low-fat vanilla frozen yogurt
1 cup frozen raspberries
2 tablespoons ground flaxseed

Nutrition Information

Calories 418	Fat 11 g	Fiber 17 g
Carbohydrates 60 g	Omega-3 Fats 3804 mg	Calcium 564 mg
Protein 22 g	Cholesterol 10 mg	Sodium 212 mg

Choco-Berry Surprise
Yield: 1 ¾ cup

1 cup vanilla soy milk, calcium enriched
1 cup frozen strawberries
2-3 tablespoons chocolate syrup

1 tablespoon flax oil

Nutrition Information

Calories 340	Fat 19 g	Fiber 7 g
Carbohydrates 40 g	Omega-3 Fats 8274 mg	Calcium 339 mg
Protein 8 g	Cholesterol 0 mg	Sodium 69 mg

Peaches & Cream
Yield: 2 cups

1 cup skim milk
1 cup low-fat vanilla frozen yogurt
1 cup peach slices, fresh or frozen
2 tablespoons ground flax

Nutrition Information

Calories 434	Fat 10 g	Fiber 8 g
Carbohydrates 68 g	Omega-3 Fats 3806 mg	Calcium 654 mg
Protein 22 g	Cholesterol 15 mg	Sodium 251 mg

Mango Shake
Yield: 2 cups

1 cup skim milk
1-1/2 cups mango slices
1/2 frozen banana, sliced
1 tablespoon flax oil
1 tablespoon ground flaxseed

Nutrition Information

Calories 452	Fat 18 g	Fiber 8 g
Carbohydrates 66 g	Omega-3 Fats 10,012 mg	Calcium 348 mg
Protein 12 g	Cholesterol 5 mg	Sodium 136 mg

Julie's Breakfast Smoothie
Yield: 3 cups

Our friend Julie (who gave us that great Cream of Mushroom Soup, earlier), has been concocting her own smoothies back in Pittsburg, Pennsylvania. Here's one she recommends.

1-1/4 cups skim milk
1 frozen banana, sliced
1 cup fresh or frozen strawberries
1/2 cup yogurt(use your favorite flavor)
2 tablespoons ground flaxseed

Nutrition Information

Calories 399	Fat 10 g	Fiber 11 g
Carbohydrates 59 g	Omega-3 Fats 3969 mg	Calcium 668 mg
Protein 22 g	Cholesterol 14 mg	Sodium 254 mg

Millie's Meal-In-A-Glass
Yield: 2 ½ cups

This smoothie comes from my friend Millie, who appeared in my first book (*Flax Your Way to Better Health*). She's been drinking this concoction for ages, and credits it with reducing her overall cholesterol from 248 to 163 (that's a 34 percent drop!!!). Even better, she has cut her LDL cholesterol from 157 to 96, and her triglycerides have fallen a whopping 70 percent, from 181 to 53! No wonder she swears by it!

1 – 11 ounce can meal replacement, any flavor
4 to 6 ounces of V-8 Splash or Diet V-8 Splash
2 tablespoons ground flaxseed
10 or more ice cubes

Nutrition Information

Calories 356	Fat 11 g	Fiber 4 g
Carbohydrates 49 g	Omega-3 Fats 3800 mg	Calcium 299 mg
Protein 15 g	Cholesterol 7 mg	Sodium 580 mg

Granola Shake
Yield: 2 cups

1 cup skim milk
1/2 cup nonfat yogurt, vanilla or flavor of choice
1 frozen banana, cut into pieces
1/4 cup cinnamon walnut granola (recipe, page 214)

Nutrition Information

Calories 364	Fat 7 g	Fiber 4 g
Carbohydrates 59 g	Omega-3 Fats 780 mg	Calcium 564 mg
Protein 19 g	Cholesterol 7 mg	Sodium 229 mg

Marge's Protein Shake
Yield: 3 ½ cups

This smoothie comes from Marge Rudisill, of Erie, Illinois. She's been a fan of flax for some time now, and this is one of her favorite ways to make sure she gets her daily allotment! Marge's motto—"If I can help somebody along life's way, then my living is all worthwhile."

2-1/4 cups rice dream beverage
1 cup fresh or frozen strawberries
1 small sliced banana
2 tablespoons protein powder
1 tablespoon ground flax
1/2 teaspoon sesame seeds

Nutrition Information

Calories 530	Fat 10 g	Fiber 10 g
Carbohydrates 97 g	Omega-3 Fats 2068 mg	Calcium 188 mg
Protein 15 g	Cholesterol 0 mg	Sodium 320 mg

Chocolate Mint
Yield: 2 cups

1 cup skim milk
2-3 tablespoons chocolate syrup
3 drops mint or peppermint extract
1/2 cup crushed ice
1 tablespoon flax oil

Nutrition Information

Calories 292	Fat 14 g	Fiber 1 g
Carbohydrates 34 g	Omega-3 Fats 8004 mg	Calcium 307 mg
Protein 9 g	Cholesterol 5 mg	Sodium 164 mg

Orange Dream
Yield: 2 ½ cups

1 cup skim milk
3 tablespoons frozen orange juice concentrate , unsweetened
1/2 cup vanilla low-fat frozen yogurt
2 tablespoons ground flaxseed

Nutrition Information

Calories 344	Fat 8 g	Fiber 5 g
Carbohydrates 51 g	Omega-3 Fats 3811 mg	Calcium 510 mg
Protein 17 g	Cholesterol 10 mg	Sodium 194 mg

Chocolate Peanut Butter Blast
Yield: 2 cups

1 cup skim milk
1 cup vanilla low-fat frozen yogurt
2 tablespoons cocoa powder, unsweetened

2 tablespoons ground flaxseed
2 tablespoons homemade flax-enriched nut butter (recipe page 121)

Nutrition Information

Calories 560	Fat 26 g	Fiber 11 g
Carbohydrates 61 g	Omega-3 Fats 4288 mg	Calcium 680 mg
Protein 30 g	Cholesterol 15 mg	Sodium 256 mg

T.J.'s Power Drink
Yield: 1 ½ cups

My oldest son, T.J., came up with this great smoothie recipe. It really packs a high-protein punch!

¼ cup skim milk
1/2 cup low- fat yogurt
1 cup fruit
1/3 cup whey protein powder
2 tablespoons ground flaxseed
1 to 2 tablespoons honey (if desired)

Nutrition Information

Calories 301	Fat 10 g	Fiber 8 g
Carbohydrates 24 g	Omega-3 Fats 3931 mg	Calcium 360 mg
Protein 29 g	Cholesterol 9 mg	Sodium 190 mg

Mike's Basic Fruit and Veggie Smoothie
Yield: 2 cups

My husband (like lots of people) all too often skips his fruits and veggies. It turns out, though, that when they're converted to liquid form, he's more than willing to drink his fill. For those of you who are new to veggie-based smoothies, you may find it best to start out with just one carrot in the mixture. The flavor can be intense!

2 oranges
2 apples

1 to 2 carrots
2 tablespoons ground flaxseed

Use your juicing machine to liquify the fruits and veggies for your base, then add the flaxseed and you're ready to roll! This makes a great base, to which you can add all sorts of extras!

Nutrition Information

Calories 402	Fat 8 g	Fiber 19 g
Carbohydrates 84 g	Omega-3 Fats 3876 mg	Calcium 202 mg
Protein 7 g	Cholesterol 0 mg	Sodium 16 mg

The Salad Bowl

13

Lots of us have gotten into the habit of dining "lite" at lunch time—and this is especially true for those of us who juggle career and family. For us, the mid-day meal of first choice is the salad. With this in mind, we went into the kitchen to come up with a batch of quick and easy single-serving salads that can be assembled in less than 15 minutes, although some of them include special "extras" that might add a bit to the prep time. Try 'em all—we're pretty sure you'll be impressed.

Taco Salad

1-1/2 cups shredded lettuce
2 tablespoons roasted tomato vinaigrette dressing (recipe, page 63)
1/4 cup fat free refried beans
2 ounces Mexican Flax Meat (recipe, page 187)
1/4 cup salsa
1/4 cup diced tomatoes
2 tablespoons green onion, chopped
1/4 cup tortilla chips
sour cream, optional

1. Place lettuce on large plate or bowl and toss with dressing.
2. Top with beans and meat.
3. Garnish with salsa, tomatoes, and onion.
4. Place chips around the outside of bowl or plate, and serve.

Nutrition Information

Calories 497	Fat 23 g	Fiber 17 g
Carbohydrates 56 g	Omega-3 Fats 4716 mg	Calcium 154 mg
Protein 23 g	Cholesterol 47 mg	Sodium 796 mg

Shrimp Caesar Salad

2 cups romaine lettuce, coarsely chopped
2 tablespoons caesar dressing (recipe, page 67)
3 ounces cooked salad shrimp
2 tablespoons fresh Parmesan cheese, shredded
1/4 cup black olives, sliced

1. Toss romaine lettuce with Caesar dressing in large bowl or plate.
2. Top with remaining ingredients.

Nutrition Information

Calories 306	Fat 20 g	Fiber 2 g
Carbohydrates 6 g	Omega-3 Fats 3827 mg	Calcium 318 mg
Protein 26 g	Cholesterol 141 mg	Sodium 604 mg

Oriental Salad

2 tablespoons oriental vinaigrette (recipe, page 62)
1/8 teaspoon wasabi (oriental horseradish)
1/4 teaspoon Dijon mustard
3 ounces chicken breast, cooked, diced
1 cup romaine lettuce, chopped
1/2 cup Nappa cabbage, chopped
1/2 cup iceburg lettuce, chopped
2 tablespoons minced green onion
1/2 cup rice noodles
1 teaspoon peanut sauce

1. Place oriental dressing in large bowl.
2. Add wasabi and mustard, and blend well.
3. Mix in all other ingredients and coat well.
4. Garnish with toasted flax and sesame seeds, if desired.

Nutrition Information

Calories 377	Fat 23 g	Fiber 5 g
Carbohydrates 12 g	Omega-3 Fats 5192 mg	Calcium 105 mg
Protein 31 g	Cholesterol 72 mg	Sodium 501 mg

Chicken Club

3 ounces cooked chicken, diced
1-1/2 cups iceburg lettuce, chopped
1/8 cup cooked, diced bacon
1/8 cup shredded reduced fat cheddar cheese
1/8 cup diced fresh tomato
1 tablespoon toasted flaxseed
2 tablespoons honey mustard dressing (recipe, page 66)

Toss all ingredients in large bowl or plate and serve!

Nutrition Information

Calories 370	Fat 21 g	Fiber 5 g
Carbohydrates 10 g	Omega-3 Fats 4978 mg	Calcium 126 mg
Protein 36 g	Cholesterol 82 mg	Sodium 534 mg

Blackened Southwest Chicken

1 tablespoon blackened seasoning
2 tablespoons southwestern breading (recipe, page 57)
3 ounces chicken breast, skinless, boneless
1 cup shredded romaine or iceburg lettuce

1-2 tablespoons roasted tomato vinaigrette (recipe, page 63)
1/8 cup shredded reduced fat cheddar cheese
1/8 cup shredded Monterey cheese
2 tablespoons green onions, sliced
1/4 cup roasted red pepper, sliced
1/4 cup roasted green pepper, sliced
1/4 cup salsa
1 tablespoon low-fat sour cream

1. Mix blackened seasoning with southwestern breading in a small bowl.
2. Coat chicken breast with this mixture.
3. Saute chicken in small non- stick skillet 3 minutes on each side or until done. Take off heat and set aside.
4. In medium bowl, toss lettuce with dressing. Place lettuce on plate.
5. Cut chicken into strips and add to lettuce.
6. Arrange with remaining ingredients and serve!

Nutrition Information

Calories 448	Fat 26 g	Fiber 6 g
Carbohydrates 17 g	Omega-3 Fats 4195 mg	Calcium 324 mg
Protein 38 g	Cholesterol 106 mg	Sodium 655 mg

California Mix Blend

1/2 cup raw broccoli florets (option steamed)
1/2 cup raw cauliflower florets (option steamed)
1/4 cup shredded carrots
1/2 cup edamame(fresh soybeans)
1 tablespoon toasted flaxseed
2 tablespoons toasted pine nuts
1 teaspoon toasted sunflower seeds
1/4 cup whole pitted black olives, sliced
2 tablespoons honey mustard dressing (recipe, page 66)

Toss all ingredients in bowl and serve chilled.

Nutrition Information

Calories 352	Fat 24 g	Fiber 11 g
Carbohydrates 23 g	Omega-3 Fats 5332 mg	Calcium 262 mg
Protein 17 g	Cholesterol 0 mg	Sodium 280 mg

Mediterranean Pasta Salad

6 ounces Hodgson Mill dry Flax Penne Noodles or
Homemade pasta (recipe, page 83)
1/4 cup black olives, chopped
1/4 cup calamata olives, chopped
2 to 2-1/2 ounces feta cheese, crumbled
mediterranean vinaigrette (recipe, page 65)

1. Cook Penne noodles according to directions.
2. Once noodles are drained, place in medium bowl, mix in olives
and feta cheese.
3. Add mediterranean vinaigrette, toss, and serve!

Nutrition Information Per 1/2 Cup

Calories 174	Fat 10 g	Fiber 3 g
Carbohydrates 17 g	Omega-3 Fats 2291 mg	Calcium 44 mg
Protein 4 g	Cholesterol 6 mg	Sodium 212 mg

Building a Better Breakfast

14

If you're planning on making a change for the better in your diet, it makes sense to start with breakfast, which has been called the "most important meal of the day." Whether you like your morning meal light or prefer a more substantial start to your day, we've got lots of ideas that will get you going with a bounce in your step! Here are some of our favorites.

Apple and Flax Pancakes
Preparation time: 10 minutes
Cooking time: 15 minutes
Yield: 12 pancakes

This recipe is one of many healthy items featured on the cafeteria menu at West Virginia University Hospitals in Morgantown, West Virginia. Cindy Gay, Registered Dietitian, Retail Manager, says her customers in the Health Sciences Center Cafeterias include health professionals and students who love products that are whole grain, low in fat, and have the extra health benefits.

1/2 cup whole wheat flour
3/4 cup all-purpose flour
1/3 cup ground flaxseed
3 tablespoons white sugar
1 tablespoon baking powder
1/2 teaspoon salt
1/4 teaspoon ground cinnamon
dash ground nutmeg
6-1/2 tablespoons egg substitute

1-1/4 cups skim milk
1 cup pared and shredded apple

1. In large bowl, combine flours, flax, sugar, baking powder, salt, cinnamon, and nutmeg.
2. In separate bowl, beat together egg substitute and skim milk.
3. Add liquid ingredients to the dry and stir until just combined.
4. Add shredded apple to batter and fold in.
5. On hot griddle coated with non-stick spray, pour 1/3 cup on griddle.
6. Cook pancake until bubbles appear on surface, turn over, and brown other side.

Nutrition Information Per Pancake

Calories 96	Fat 2 g	Fiber 2 g
Carbohydrates 16 g	Omega-3 Fats 859 mg	Calcium 116 mg
Protein 4 g	Cholesterol 1 mg	Sodium 249 mg

Blueberry Flax Pancakes
Preparation time: 10 minutes
Cooking time: 15 minutes
Yield: 12 pancakes

This recipe is from Peggy Foster, breast cancer survivor, who presently lives in Mequon, Wisconsin. Peggy eats flax every day, as part of her healthier approach to eating and living!

2 cups all-purpose baking mix
1-1/2 cups skim milk
1 whole egg
3/4 teaspoon ground cinnamon
1 cup ground flaxseed
1 cup blueberries, washed and drained

1. In bowl, mix all ingredients except blueberries until blended.

2. Fold in blueberries.

3. On hot griddle coated with non-stick spray, pour 1/3 cup batter for each pancake.

4. When bubbles break on surface or side is brown, turn and cook until golden brown.

5. If batter becomes too thick, add a little milk.

Nutrition Information Per Pancake

Calories 153	Fat 8 g	Fiber 3 g
Carbohydrates 16 g	Omega-3 Fats 2585 mg	Calcium 68 mg
Protein 5 g	Cholesterol 18 mg	Sodium 259 mg

Flax Buttermilk Pancakes
Preparation time: 10 minutes
Cooking time: 10 minutes
Yield: 8 pancakes

This recipe is from Joanne Shearer, who also contributed the One-Hour Flax Rolls recipe.

1 cup whole wheat flour
1/4 cup ground flaxseed
1/2 teaspoon baking soda
2 teaspoons baking powder
1/2 teaspoon salt
1 tablespoon white sugar
1 whole egg
1 cup low-fat buttermilk
1 tablespoon canola oil

1. Combine flour, flax, baking soda, baking powder, salt, and sugar in a large bowl.

2. In a separate bowl, mix egg, milk, and oil with a whisk.

3. Add liquid ingredients to dry ingredients. Gently stir until moistened. but do not overmix. Batter should be lumpy.

4. Spray a griddle or pan with non-stick spray. Cook pancakes on hot griddle.

5. Serve with fruit toppings like: sliced strawberries topped with low-fat yogurt, hot cinnamon applesauce, or peaches topped with low-fat yogurt.

Nutrition Information Per Pancake

Calories 113	Fat 5 g	Fiber 3 g
Carbohydrates 14 g	Omega-3 Fats 1142 mg	Calcium 121 mg
Protein 5 g	Cholesterol 28 mg	Sodium 388 mg

French Toast
Preparation time: 10 minutes
Cooking time: 10 minutes
Yield: 6 slices

2 eggs, slightly beaten
1 tablespoon white sugar
1/4 teaspoon salt
1/4 teaspoon cinnamon, if desired
1/2 cup skim milk
6 slices flax-based bread (see Chapter 15 for home-made bread recipes, or use store-bought bread)
Powdered sugar, as desired

1. Heat griddle to medium heat.
2. In bowl, combine all ingredients, except bread, and mix well.
3. Coat griddle w/ non-stick spray.
4. Dip bread in egg mixture, turning to coat both sides.
5. Cook on griddle over medium heat, about 4 minutes, or until brown.
6. Sprinkle with powdered sugar or other toppings as desired.

Nutrition Information Per Slice

Calories 150	Fat 6 g	Fiber 3 g
Carbohydrates 17 g	Omega-3 Fats 1934 mg	Calcium 58 mg
Protein 7 g	Cholesterol 73 mg	Sodium 276 mg

Flax Waffles

Preparation time: 10 minutes
Cooking time: 15 minutes
Yield: 12 - 6 inch waffles

1-1/4 cups all-purpose flour
3/4 cup ground flaxseed
1 tablespoon baking powder
1 tablespoon white sugar
1/4 teaspoon salt
3 large eggs, well beaten
1/4 cup canola oil
1-1/2 cups skim milk

1. Preheat waffle iron.
2. In large bowl, mix together flour, flax, baking powder, sugar, and salt.
3. In separate bowl, whisk together eggs, oil, and milk.
4. Mix together liquid ingredients into dry ingredients.
5. Spoon amount of batter recommended by waffle iron's manufacturer onto hot iron.
6. Close lid and bake until the waffle is golden brown.
7. Serve with powdered sugar or other favorite toppings.

Nutrition Information Per Waffle

Calories 152	Fat 9 g	Fiber 3 g
Carbohydrates 13 g	Omega-3 Fats 2361 mg	Calcium 131 mg
Protein 5 g	Cholesterol 36 mg	Sodium 200 mg

Flax Coffeecake

Preparation time: 15 minutes
Cooking time: 25-30 minutes
Yield: 16 pieces

1 cup ground flaxseed
1/2 cup all-purpose flour
2/3 cup brown sugar, packed
1/2 cup quick cooking oats
1/3 cup canola oil
1 teaspoon baking powder
1/4 teaspoon baking soda
1/2 teaspoon ground cinnamon
1/8 teaspoon salt
1/4 teaspoon ground nutmeg
1/2 cup low-fat buttermilk
2 whole eggs
1/3 cup chopped walnuts

1. Preheat oven to 375 F.
2. In large bowl, combine flax, flour, sugar, and oats. Cut in oil until particles are small. Set aside ½ cup of this mixture for topping.
3. In crumb mixture, add remaining ingredients, except nuts, and mix well.
4. Pour batter in 8 or 9 inch square or round pan(coated with non-stick spray).
5. Sprinkle with reserved crumbs and nuts.
6. Bake for 25 to 30 minutes, until toothpick put in center comes out clean.

Nutrition Information Per Piece

Calories 153	Fat 9 g	Fiber 3 g
Carbohydrates 14 g	Omega-3 Fats 2439 mg	Calcium 60 mg
Protein 4 g	Cholesterol 27 mg	Sodium 82 mg

Sticky Cinnamon Rolls
Preparation time: 12-14 hours
Cooking time: 20-25 minutes
Yield: 16 rolls

These are a real breakfast favorite in my house. I find it convenient to do most of the prep work the night before, so that all I've got to do in the morning is pop them into the oven.

1 package (2-1/4 teaspoons) active dry yeast
1/4 cup warm (105-115 F) water
1/2 cup all-purpose flour
1 cup ground flaxseed
1/3 cup white sugar
1/4 teaspoon salt
2 large eggs, lightly beaten
1/4 cup skim milk
1 teaspoon vanilla
1-1/3 to 1-1/2 cups bread flour
2 tablespoons unsalted butter, softened.

1. Combine yeast and water in a heavy duty mixer or large mixing bowl until yeast is dissolved.
2. Add flour, flax, sugar, salt, eggs, milk, and vanilla. Mix on low speed or mix by hand until blended.
3. Gradually stir or mix in bread flour until dough is formed.
4. Knead by hand on floured board or knead with a dough hook on low to medium speed for 5-7 minutes until the dough is smooth and elastic, and no longer sticks to your hands or the bowl.
5. Knead in the butter until incorporated completely.
6. Place the dough in a large bowl that has been coated with non-stick spray or small amount of oil.
7. Cover with plastic wrap and let rise in a warm place until doubled in volume, about 1-1/2 hours.
8. Punch down the dough, knead briefly, and refrigerate covered, until dough has doubled in volume again. This takes between 4 and 12 hours. (I like to let it rise overnight).

9. When ready to assemble make carmel sauce below.

Caramel sauce
2/3 cup brown sugar, packed
3 tablespoons unsalted butter
1/2 cup honey
1/3 cup chopped pecans

1. Coat 9X13 baking pan with non-stick spray.
2. Mix together brown sugar, butter and honey in saucepan. Bring to boil, stirring regularly to dissolve sugar and melt butter.
3. Remove from heat and fold in pecans.
4. Pour hot syrup in baking pan and spread evenly. Set aside.

10. Punch down the dough.
11. Roll out dough on floured board using a rolling pin into a 12 X 16 rectangle.
12. Sprinkle with mixture of 1/4 cup brown sugar (packed) and 1 tablespoon ground cinnamon.
13. Roll up the dough as you would a jelly roll.
14. Cut crosswise into 16 slices.
15. Put slices in pan, cover with plastic wrap, and let rise at room temperature until doubled in volume, about 1 hour.
16. Preheat oven to 350 F.
17. Bake uncovered until golden brown, about 20-25 minutes.
18. Let rolls cool in pan for a few minutes, then invert the pan onto a baking sheet lined with aluminum foil. Serve warm.

Nutrition Information Per Roll

Calories 246	Fat 10 g	Fiber 3 g
Carbohydrates 36 g	Omega-3 Fats 2017 mg	Calcium 42 mg
Protein 5 g	Cholesterol 36 mg	Sodium 55 mg

Cinnamon Scones
Preparation time: 20 minutes
Cooking time: 12-15 minutes
Yield: 28 scones

1 cup ground flaxseed
1 cup low-fat buttermilk
1 cup raisins
1-3/4 cups whole wheat flour
4 teaspoons baking powder
3 tablespoons brown sugar
salt, to taste
2 teaspoons cinnamon
1/3 cup unsalted butter

1. Preheat oven to 425 F.
2. Combine flaxseed, raisins, and buttermilk in small bowl.
3. In separate bowl, combine dry ingredients together. Cut in butter.
4. Combine liquid ingredients with dry ingredients. Work into a soft dough.
5. Divide into two parts and pat out into a floured board to ½" thickness.
6. Cut each piece into triangles, squares, or rounds, depending on your preference.
7. Bake for 12-15 minutes, until slightly brown. Test for doneness by pressing finger in center of scone—if the dough pops back up, the scones are done.

Nutrition Information Per Scone

Calories 93	Fat 4 g	Fiber 3 g
Carbohydrates 12 g	Omega-3 Fats 1140 mg	Calcium 69 mg
Protein 3 g	Cholesterol 6 mg	Sodium 82 mg

Cinnamon Walnut Granola
Preparation time: 5 minutes
Cooking time: 35 minutes
Yield: 25 - ½ cup servings

Here's another contribution from Joanne Shearer. She's a real pro when it comes to cooking with flax! She mentions that you can add raisins or dates to the basic recipe for a little extra goodness.

7-1/2 cups old fashioned oatmeal
1 cup walnuts, chopped
1 cup shredded coconut
1/2 cup ground flaxseed
1/2 cup brown sugar
1/2 cup canola oil
1/2 cup honey
1/2 tablespoon cinnamon
1 tablespoon vanilla

1. Preheat oven to 275 F.
2. In mixer bowl, combine oats, coconut, nuts, and ground flaxseed.
3. In microwavable bowl, blend together brown sugar, oil, honey, cinnamon, and vanilla. Cook on high in microwave until mixture starts bubbling.
4. Pour over oat mixture and mix well.
5. Thinly spread on baking sheet.
6. Bake for 15 minutes. Stir, return to oven for additional 15 minutes or until oats are toasted.
7. Cool thoroughly. Store in airtight container.

Nutrition Information Per 1/2 Cup

Calories 233	Fat 11 g	Fiber 4 g
Carbohydrates 29 g	Omega-3 Fats 1483 mg	Calcium 30 mg
Protein 5 g	Cholesterol 0 mg	Sodium 14 mg

Quiche

Preparation time: 20 minutes
Baking time: 40-45 minutes
Yield: 8 servings

Crust
¾ cup all-purpose flour
¾ cup ground flaxseed
1/8 teaspoon salt
1/3 cup canola oil
¼ cup skim milk

Filling
1 tablespoon unsalted butter
8 ounces fresh mushrooms, washed, sliced
2 scallions, minced
½ garlic clove, minced
¾ teaspoon oregano
¾ teaspoon basil
¼ teaspoon salt
¼ teaspoon marjoram
1/8 teaspoon black pepper
1/8 teaspoon dry mustard
4 whole eggs
¾ cup skim milk

1. In bowl, mix together flour, flax, and salt.
2. In separate bowl, whisk together oil and milk.
3. Mix liquid ingredients with dry ingredients.
4. Place in 9 inch pie crust(coasted with non-stick spray) and using fingers press in dough. Set aside.
5. Preheat oven to 375 F.
6. In large skillet over medium heat, melt butter. Add mushrooms, scallions, and garlic and sauté for a few minutes. Add seasonings and cook for another few minutes until mushrooms are cooked. Set aside.
7. In a medium bowl, combine eggs with milk and beat well.

8. Stir in mushroom mixture and pour into pie crust.

9. Bake until filling is puffed, set and starting to brown—about 40-45 minutes.

Nutrition Information Per Serving

Calories 250	Fat 18 g	Fiber 4 g
Carbohydrates 12 g	Omega-3 Fats 3783 mg	Calcium 90 mg
Protein 9 g	Cholesterol 111 mg	Sodium 146 mg

Breads & Muffins

15

We've come up with a batch of tasty baked-goods for you to try. Let's start off with the ones we've developed that take advantage of those popular bread-making machines.

Juanita's Flaxseed Sandwich Bread
Yield: 1 ½ pound loaf (14 slices)

This recipe comes from Juanita Nerstheimer, of Sterling, Illinois. Juanita started adding flaxseed to her diet after reading my first book, *Flax Your Way to Better Health*. As an LPN for 36 years and battling mercury poisoning, as well as many other allergies, she started making drastic changes to improve her health, and flaxseed has become an important element of her diet. She reports that her flaxseed consumption has contributed dramatically to her recovery—as of May 2003, her doctor told her she was once again mercury-free and her allergies have been conquered.

1 cup plus 2 tablespoons water
1-1/2 tablespoons canola oil
3 tablespoons honey
1/2 teaspoon liquid lecithin
3 cups whole wheat flour or spelt flour
1/2 cup whole flaxseed, then grind to be coarse
2 tablespoons gluten flour
3 tablespoons powdered whey
1-1/2 teaspoons sea salt
3 teaspoons active dry yeast (use less for heavy bread)

Put all ingredients into the inner pan in the order your bread machine calls for. Select basic wheat cycle, light crust.

Nutrition Information Per Slice

Calories 152	Fat 5 g	Fiber 5 g
Carbohydrates 24 g	Omega-3 Fats 1669 mg	Calcium 40 mg
Protein 5 g	Cholesterol 0 mg	Sodium 271 mg

Naomi's Flax Bread
Yield: 2 pound loaf (16 slices)

Naomi Arens of Middle Grove, New York, swears by this recipe. She started eating flax on her doctor's recommendation, in hopes that it would help her overcome her problems with IBS (Irritable Bowel Syndrome), particularly with constipation. She also adds ground flaxseed to her morning oatmeal—and she says that it's made a big difference in her health and personal comfort.

1-1/2 cups water
1-1/2 teaspoons salt
2 tablespoons canola oil
2 tablespoons honey
2-1/2 cups bread flour
1-1/4 cups whole wheat flour
2/3 cup quick cooking oats
2-1/4 teaspoons active dry yeast
1/4 cup ground flaxseed
2 tablespoons sunflower seeds

Put all ingredients into the inner pan in the order your bread machine calls for. Select basic wheat cycle.

Nutrition Information Per Slice

Calories 162	Fat 4 g	Fiber 3 g
Carbohydrates 27 g	Omega-3 Fats 662 mg	Calcium 14 mg
Protein 5 g	Cholesterol 0 mg	Sodium 220 mg

Best of Both Worlds Flax Bread
Yield: 1 ½ pound loaf(14 slices)

This recipe is from Diane Morris, a Registered Dietitian living in Toronto, Canada. Diane loves to make this recipe at least once a month. Her favorite way to serve it is toasted and slathered with a small amount of ground flax mixed with honey.

1-1/4 cups low-fat buttermilk
2 tablespoons margarine(trans-fat free)
1-3/4 cups all-purpose flour
1 cup whole wheat flour
1/3 cup ground flaxseed
2 tablespoons wheat bran
2 tablespoons rolled oats
1 tablespoon whole flaxseed
3 tablespoons white sugar
2 teaspoons baking powder
1/2 teaspoon baking soda
3/4 teaspoon salt
1 teaspoon gluten
2 teaspoons active dry yeast

Place these ingredients in the bread machine in the order shown. Use basic bread, light crust setting.

Nutrition Information Per Slice

Calories 139	Fat 3 g	Fiber 3 g
Carbohydrates 23 g	Omega-3 Fats 914 mg	Calcium 80 mg
Protein 5 g	Cholesterol 1 mg	Sodium 284 mg

Homemade Yeast Breads

While bread-making machines are convenient, some of us like good, old-fashioned baking days. If that's your style, here are some recipes that call for traditional methods. Enjoy!

White Bread Plus
Preparation time: 1 hour 20 minutes
Baking time: 40 minutes
Yield: makes one 8 ½ X 4 ½ inch loaf (16 slices)

In this case, the plus is—of course—flax. This is a nice, basic bread for sandwiches or toast.

1-1/2 cups bread flour
1 cup ground flaxseed
1 tablespoon white sugar
1 package (2-1/4 teaspoons) quick-rising active dry yeast
1 teaspoon salt
1 cup warm water (115 to 125 F)
1 tablespoon unsalted butter, melted
3/4 cup bread flour

1. Stir together in large mixing bowl or in the bowl of a heavy-duty mixer bread flour, flaxseed, sugar, yeast, and salt.
2. Add water and butter. Mix for about 1 minute.
3. Gradually add bread flour until the dough is moist, but not sticky.
4. Knead for about 10 minutes by hand on floured table, or with the dough hook on low/medium speed until the dough is smooth and elastic.
5. Transfer the dough to an oiled bowl, cover with plastic wrap, and let rise in a warm place until doubled in volume, 30-45 minutes.
6. Coat 8 ½ X 4 ½ inch loaf pan with non-stick spray. Punch the dough down, form it into a loaf, and place seam side down in the pan. Cover with plastic wrap and let rise in a warm place until doubled in volume, 30 to 45 minutes.

7. Preheat oven to 450 F while dough is rising.

8. After dough has doubled in volume, bake the loaf for about 10 minutes.

9. Reduce the heat to 350 F and bake for about 30 minutes.

10. Remove the loaf from the pan to a rack and let cool completely before cutting.

Nutrition Information Per Slice

Calories 117	Fat 4 g	Fiber 3 g
Carbohydrates 15 g	Omega-3 Fats 1948 mg	Calcium 23 mg
Protein 4 g	Cholesterol 2 mg	Sodium 149 mg

Whole Wheat Bread with Flax

Preparation time: 1 hour 20 minutes
Cooking time: 40 minutes
Yield: makes one 8 ½ X 4 ½ inch loaf (16 slices)

3/4 cup bread flour
3/4 cup whole wheat flour
1 cup ground flaxseed
1 tablespoon white sugar
1 package (2-1/4 teaspoons) quick-rising active dry yeast
1 teaspoon salt
1 cup warm water (115 to 125 F)
1 tablespoon unsalted butter, melted
3/4 cup bread flour

1. Stir together in large mixing bowl or in the bowl of a heavy-duty mixer bread flour, whole wheat flour, flaxseed, sugar, yeast, and salt.

2. Add water and butter. Mix for about 1 minute.

3. Gradually add bread flour until the dough is moist, but not sticky.

4. Knead for about 10 minutes by hand on floured table, or with the dough hook on low/medium speed until the dough is smooth and elastic.

5. Transfer the dough to an oiled bowl, cover with plastic wrap, and let rise in a warm place until doubled in volume, 30-45 minutes.
6. Coat 8 ½ X 4 ½ inch loaf pan with non-stick spray. Punch the dough down, form it into a loaf, and place seam side down in the pan. Cover with plastic wrap and let rise in a warm place until doubled in volume, 30 to 45 minutes.
7. Preheat oven to 450 F while dough is rising.
8. After dough has doubled in volume, bake the loaf for about 10 minutes.
9. Reduce the heat to 350 F and bake for about 30 minutes.
10. Remove loaf from pan to a rack and let cool completely.

Nutrition Information Per Slice

Calories 113	Fat 4 g	Fiber 3 g
Carbohydrates 14 g	Omega-3 Fats 1948 mg	Calcium 24 mg
Protein 4 g	Cholesterol 2 mg	Sodium 149 mg

Quickbreads, Muffins, and Other Bakery Delights

Why stop with breads? If you've got the baking bug, there are lots of other goodies you can make for yourself and your family. Here are just a few.

One Hour Flax Rolls
Preparation time: 40 minutes
Baking time: 12 minutes
Yield: 18 rolls

This recipe comes from Joanne Shearer, a Registered Dietitian working at the Heart Hospital of South Dakota. This 55 bed state of the art cardiovascular facility opened in March 2001, and its Food and Nutrition Service promotes a healthy food culture by incorporating a modified Mediterranean diet into their menu plans. Flax is incorporated into most of the baked products they serve to both their patients and café' customers.

1 cup skim milk
1/2 cup water
1-1/2 cups whole wheat flour
2 cups all-purpose flour
1/2 cup ground flaxseed
3 tablespoons white sugar
2 packages(1 tablespoon + 1-1/2 teaspoons) active dry yeast
1 teaspoon salt

1. In a 2 cup glass measuring cup, combine milk and water. Microwave until very warm (120-130 F).
2. In mixer bowl, combine all remaining ingredients and mix thoroughly.
3. Add dough hook to mixer. Gradually add warm liquids to flour mixture. If needed, add more flour until dough pulls away from the sides of the bowl. Kneed on low to medium speed for 2 minutes.
4. Place in greased bowl, cover with towel, and let rise in warm area for about 15 minutes.
5. Punch down. Shape rolls as desired and place in pan sprayed with non-stick cooking spray.
6. Preheat oven 425 F.
7. Let rise in warm area for 15 minutes.
8. Bake for about 12 minutes or until golden brown.
9. Remove from pan and let cook on rack.

Nutrition Information Per Roll

Calories 117	Fat 2 g	Fiber 3 g
Carbohydrates 21 g	Omega-3 Fats 865 mg	Calcium 32 mg
Protein 4 g	Cholesterol 0 mg	Sodium 139 mg

Cornbread
Preparation time: 15 minutes
Baking time: 20 minutes
Yield: 16 pieces

My husband Mike is a big cornbread fan, and this is one of his favorite treats.

1/2 cup ground flaxseed
1-1/4 cups cornmeal
1/2 cup all-purpose flour
4 tablespoons white sugar
2 teaspoons baking powder
1/2 teaspoon baking soda
1/2 teaspoon salt
2 large eggs
2/3 cup skim milk
2/3 cup low-fat buttermilk
2 tablespoons canola oil

1. Preheat oven to 425 F.
2. Spray a 9 X 9 inch pan with non-stick spray.
3. In large bowl, mix together flaxseed, cornmeal, flour, sugar, baking powder, baking soda, and salt.
4. In another bowl, whisk together eggs, milk, and buttermilk.
5. Add the wet ingredients to the dry ingredients and stir until moistened.
6. Fold in canola oil.
7. Scrape the batter into the pan and spread evenly. Bake for about 20 minutes, until a toothpick inserted in the center comes out clean.

Nutrition Information Per Piece

Calories 116	Fat 4 g	Fiber 2 g
Carbohydrates 15 g	Omega-3 Fats 1137 mg	Calcium 109 mg
Protein 4 g	Cholesterol 27 mg	Sodium 344 mg

Lemon Poppy Seed Bread
Preparation time: 15 minutes
Baking time: 40-45 minutes
Yield: 16 slices

1-1/4 cups all-purpose flour

3/4 cup ground flaxseed
1/4 cup white sugar
1 teaspoon baking powder
1/2 teaspoon baking soda
1/4 teaspoon salt
1 tablespoon lemon juice
1 egg
1 cup low-fat buttermilk
1/4 cup canola oil
1 tablespoon grated lemon zest
1-1/2 tablespoons poppyseed

1. Preheat oven to 350 F.
2. In large bowl, mix flour, flax, sugar, baking powder, baking soda, and salt.
3. In separate bowl, mix together egg, lemon juice, buttermilk, and canola oil.
4. Add wet ingredients to dry ingredients until moistened.
5. Fold in lemon zest and poppseed.
6. Coat 8 ½ X 4 ½ inch loaf pan with non-stick spray.
7. Place batter in pan and bake for 40-45 minutes, until golden brown or a toothpick inserted in the center comes out clean. Let cool in the pan on a rack for at least 10-15 minutes before unmolding to cool completely on the rack.

Nutrition Information Per Slice

Calories 121	Fat 7 g	Fiber 2 g
Carbohydrates 12 g	Omega-3 Fats 1773 mg	Calcium 64 mg
Protein 3 g	Cholesterol 14 mg	Sodium 129 mg

Date-Nut Bread
Preparation time: 15 minutes
Baking time: 50 minutes
Yield: 18 slices

I modified my grandmother's traditional date-nut bread recipe to come up with this one. I'm proud to say that this "new-fangled" adaptation has become a family favorite.

1-1/2 cups chopped dates
1 teaspoon baking soda
1 cup boiling water
1-1/4 cups all-purpose flour
3/4 cup ground flaxseed
1/4 teaspoon salt
1/2 teaspoon baking powder
2/3 cup light or dark brown sugar, packed
2 large eggs
1/4 cup canola oil
1 teaspoon vanilla
½ cup chopped walnuts

1. Preheat oven to 350 F.
2. In medium bowl, place dates. Stir together boiling water and baking soda and pour over dates. Let stand until mixture is lukewarm or until dates are softened, about 10-15 minutes.
3. In different bowl, mix together flour, flax, salt, sugar, and baking powder.
4. In separate bowl, mix together eggs, oil, and vanilla.
5. Add date mixture(including liquid) to wet mixture.
6. Stir flour mixture into liquid ingredients until blended.
7. Fold in chopped walnuts.
8. Coat 9 X 5 inch loaf pan with non-stick spray and pour in batter.
9. Bake for about 50 minutes until dark brown, or until a toothpick inserted in the center comes out clean. Let cool in the pan on a rack for at least 10-15 minutes before unmolding to cool completely on the rack.

Nutrition Information Per Slice

Calories 179	Fat 8 g	Fiber 3 g
Carbohydrates 24 g	Omega-3 Fats 1877 mg	Calcium 39 mg
Protein 3 g	Cholesterol 24 mg	Sodium 128 mg

Pumpkin Date Bread
Preparation time: 15 minutes
Baking time: 55 minutes
Yield: 18 slices

1 cup all-purpose flour
3/4 cup ground flaxseed
1-1/2 teaspoons ground cinnamon
1 teaspoon baking soda
1/2 teaspoon salt
1 teaspoon ground ginger
1/2 teaspoon ground nutmeg
1/4 teaspoon ground cloves
1/4 teaspoon baking powder
2/3 cup white sugar
1/4 cup skim milk
1/2 teaspoon vanilla
1/4 cup canola oil
1 large egg
1 cup pumpkin puree(could also use cooked mashed squash, yams,
or sweet potatoes)
1/3 cup chopped walnuts or pecans
1/3 cup chopped dates

1. Preheat oven to 350 F.
2. In large bowl, mix together flour, flax, spices, salt, sugar, baking soda, and baking powder.
3. In separate bowl, mix together well milk, vanilla, oil, egg, and pumpkin.
4. Mix wet ingredients into dry ingredients until moistened.
5. Fold in dates and chopped nuts.
6. Coat 9 X 5 loaf pan with non-stick spray.
7. Pour batter in pan. Bake for about 55 minutes until dark brown, or until a toothpick inserted in the center comes out clean. Let cool in the pan on a rack for at least 10-15 minutes before unmolding to cool completely on the rack.

Nutrition Information Per Slice

Calories 140	Fat 7 g	Fiber 3 g
Carbohydrates 17 g	Omega-3 Fats 1774 mg	Calcium 33 mg
Protein 3 g	Cholesterol 12 mg	Sodium 150 mg

Banana Bread
Preparation time: 15 minutes
Baking time: 50-55 minutes
Yield: 16 slices

One of my favorite childhood memories is the delicious smell of my mother's banana bread as it baked. I've made a few minor changes to my mom's original recipe, and I hope your family likes it as much as mine does.

1-1/4 cups all-purpose flour
3/4 cup ground flaxseed
2/3 cup white sugar
2 teaspoons baking powder
1/4 teaspoon salt
2 eggs
1/4 cup skim milk
1/4 cup canola oil
1 cup mashed bananas(about 3 medium or 2 large)
1/2 teaspoon vanilla
1/3 cup chopped walnuts

1. Preheat oven to 350 F.
2. In large bowl, mix flour, flax, sugar, baking powder, and salt together.
3. In food processor or bowl, mash bananas. Then add eggs, milk, oil, and vanilla, and mix in well together.
4. Mix wet ingredients into dry ingredients just until moistened.
5. Fold in chopped nuts.
6. Coat 8 ½ X 4 ½ inch loaf pan with non-stick spray.

7. Pour batter in loaf pan. Bake for about 50-55 minutes until dark brown, or until a toothpick inserted in the center comes out clean. Let cool in the pan on a rack for at least 10-15 minutes before unmolding to cool completely on the rack.

Nutrition Information Per Slice

Calories 166	Fat 8 g	Fiber 2 g
Carbohydrates 20 g	Omega-3 Fats 2000 mg	Calcium 61 mg
Protein 4 g	Cholesterol 27 mg	Sodium 110 mg

Zucchini Bread
Preparation time: 15 minutes
Baking time: 50-55 minutes
Yield: 16 slices

I grew up on a farm in Wisconsin, and we grew lots of zucchini—so it's no wonder that we'd come up with a pretty great zucchini bread recipe. Here's my old family favorite, with a flaxseed twist!

2/3 cup white sugar
1-1/4 cups all-purpose flour
3/4 cup ground flaxseed
1/4 teaspoon salt
1/2 teaspoon baking soda
2 teaspoons baking powder
1-1/2 teaspoons cinnamon
1/3 cup canola oil
1 whole egg
1 cup grated zucchini
1-1/2 teaspoons vanilla

1. Preheat oven to 350 F.
2. In large bowl, mix together sugar, flour, flax, salt, baking soda, baking powder, and cinnamon.

3. In separate bowl or food processor, combine grated zucchini, egg, oil, and vanilla.

4. Mix wet ingredients with dry ingredients until moistened.

5. Coat 8 ½ X 4 ½ inch loaf pan with non-stick spray.

6. Pour batter in loaf pan. Bake for about 50-55 minutes until dark brown, or until a toothpick inserted in the center comes out clean. Let cool in the pan on a rack for at least 10-15 minutes before unmolding to cool completely on the rack.

Nutrition Information Per Slice

Calories 142	Fat 7 g	Fiber 2 g
Carbohydrates 16 g	Omega-3 Fats 1873 mg	Calcium 55 mg
Protein 3 g	Cholesterol 13 mg	Sodium 143 mg

Banana Chocolate Flax Muffins
Preparation time: 15 minutes
Baking time: 20-25 minutes
Yield: 12 muffins

My sister, Rosie, designed this recipe for her husband, Jerome, who loves chocolate, and consumes flax daily for heart health. She says that if you're cutting back on chocolate, just substitute a half-cup of blueberries for the mini chocolate chips. The muffins will still taste great!

1-1/2 cups all-purpose flour
3/4 cup ground flaxseed
2/3 cup white sugar
1 teaspoon baking soda
1 whole egg
1/4 cup canola oil
1 cup mashed bananas (3 medium or 2 large)
1 teaspoon vanilla
2 tablespoons low-fat sour cream
1/2 cup mini chocolate chips

1. Preheat oven to 350 F.

2. In large bowl, mix together flour, flaxseed, sugar, and baking soda.
3. In separate bowl or food processor, mix together egg, canola oil, bananas, vanilla, and sour cream.
4. Mix wet ingredients to dry ingredients until moistened.
5. Fold in chocolate chips.
6. Coat muffin tin with non-stick spray. Pour batter into muffin tin.
7. Bake for 20-25 minutes or until golden brown.

Nutrition Information Per Muffin

Calories 222	Fat 10 g	Fiber 3 g
Carbohydrates 30 g	Omega-3 Fats 2365 mg	Calcium 30 mg
Protein 4 g	Cholesterol 19 mg	Sodium 116 mg

Cindy's Flax Muffins
Preparation time: 15 minutes
Baking time: 15-20 minutes
Yield: 18 muffins

This is one of the many healthy recipes featured on the cafeteria menu at West Virginia University Hospitals in Morgantown, West Virginia. Cindy Gay, Registered Dietitian, Retail Manager, says her customers in the Health Sciences Center Cafeterias include health professionals and students who love products that are whole grain, and low in fat, and they're becoming big fans of flaxseed!

1/2 cup whole wheat flour
1 cup all-purpose flour
3/4 cup ground flaxseed
3/4 cup oat bran
1/2 cup brown sugar, packed
2 teaspoons baking soda
1 teaspoon baking powder
1/4 teaspoon salt
2 teaspoons ground cinnamon
1-1/2 cups shredded carrots
1 cup pineapple tidbits, drained
1/2 cup raisins

1/3 cup plus 1 tablespoon egg substitute
2 tablespoons unsweetened applesauce
1 teaspoon vanilla
1 cup skim milk
1 tablespoon lemon juice

1. Preheat oven to 350 F.
2. In large bowl, mix flours, flax, oat bran, brown sugar, baking soda, baking powder, salt, and cinnamon.
3. Stir in carrots, pineapple, and raisins.
4. Combine eggs, milk, lemon juice, applesauce, and vanilla in separate bowl.
5. Add liquids to dry ingredients, stir until moist (batter will be lumpy).
6. Coat muffin tin with non-stick spray. Pour batter in tins.
7. Bake for 15-20 minutes, or until golden brown.

Nutrition Information Per Muffin

Calories 127	Fat 3 g	Fiber 4 g
Carbohydrates 23 g	Omega-3 Fats 1311 mg	Calcium 66 mg
Protein 4 g	Cholesterol 0 mg	Sodium 224 mg

Multi-Grain Pumpkin Muffins
Preparation time: 15 minutes
Baking time: 15-20 minutes
Yield: 12 muffins

Cindy Gay sends us this recipe, too. This one is a real crowd-pleaser.

1/2 cup whole wheat flour
1 cup all-purpose flour
3/4 cup ground flaxseed
3/4 cup dry cooking oats
1/2 cup brown sugar, packed
2 teaspoons baking soda

1 teaspoon baking powder
1/4 teaspoon salt
2 teaspoons cinnamon
½ cup raisins
1 cup pureed pumpkin (fresh or canned)
1/3 cup plus 1 tablespoon egg substitute
2 tablespoons unsweetened applesauce
1 teaspoon vanilla
1 cup skim milk
1 tablespoon lemon juice

1. Preheat oven to 350 F.
2. In large bowl, mix together flours, flax, oats, brown sugar, baking soda, baking powder, salt, cinnamon, and raisins.
3. Combine eggs, pumpkin, milk, applesauce, lemon juice, and vanilla in separate bowl.
4. Add liquid ingredients to dry mixture, stir until moist(batter will be lumpy).
5. Coat muffin tin with non-stick spray.
6. Pour batter in tins. Bake for 15-20 minutes, or until golden brown.

Nutrition Information Per Muffin

Calories 189	Fat 4 g	Fiber 5 g
Carbohydrates 33 g	Omega-3 Fats 1956 mg	Calcium 98 mg
Protein 6 g	Cholesterol 0 mg	Sodium 331 mg

Sue's Applesauce Muffins
Preparation time: 15 minutes
Baking time: 15-20 minutes
Yield: 12 muffins

This recipe is from Sue Cole Staley, Moline, Illinois. George, her husband, read several articles touting the benefits of eating flax—especially for women. Because he intends for Sue to stick around a long time, he purchased some flax and began experimenting. Now they both look for ways to incorporate flax in their diets.

1/2 cup raisins
1/3 cup apple juice concentrate
2 ripe bananas, sliced
1/4 cup canola oil
1 teaspoon vanilla
1/2 cup unsweetened applesauce
1 whole egg
1 cup whole wheat flour
1/2 cup ground flaxseed
1/2 teaspoon baking powder
1/2 teaspoon baking soda
1/4 teaspoon salt
1 tablespoon cinnamon

1. Preheat oven to 400 F.
2. In small bowl, combine raisins and apple juice concentrate. Heat mixture in microwave for 1 -1 ½ minutes, or until raisins are soft.
3. In blender or food processor, mix bananas, oil, vanilla, applesauce, and egg.
4. In large bowl, mix together flour, flax, baking powder, baking soda, salt, and cinnamon.
5. Pour liquid mixture & raisins in dry ingredients, and blend until moistened.
6. Coat muffin tin with non-stick spray.
7. Put batter in muffin tins. Bake for 15-20 minutes, or until brown.

Nutrition Information Per Muffin

Calories 162	Fat 8 g	Fiber 4 g
Carbohydrates 22 g	Omega-3 Fats 1726 mg	Calcium 43 mg
Protein 4 g	Cholesterol 18 mg	Sodium 132 mg

Desserts & Snacks

16

We've found ways to use flax in just about everything else—so now it's time to adapt it to those sweet-tooth pleasers. Once again, the versatility of flax is obvious in the way its nutty, warm flavor complements the foods we turn to when we're looking for a special treat. And since flax is so nutritious, you can feel a little less guilty when you indulge! Just remember, a little treat is great, but you don't want to overdo it on the sweets.

Mary's Monster Bars
Preparation time: 15 minutes
Baking time: 20-25 minutes
Yield: 54 bars

Mary Flint, Registered Nurse from Morrison, Illinois, sends us this tasty treat. Go sparingly on these, however—there's lots of sugar in this one.

1 stick (1/2 cup) unsalted butter
2/3 cup brown sugar, packed
2/3 cup white sugar
2 whole eggs
1 cup peanut butter, smooth or crunchy
1 teaspoon vanilla
3 cups quick cooking oats
1 cup ground flaxseed
2 teaspoons baking powder
1/2 cup chocolate chips
1/2 cup mini M & M's

1. Preheat oven to 350 F.
2. Coat a 10 1/4 X 15 inch cookie sheet with non-stick spray.
3. Beat together butter and sugars using mixer. Add eggs, peanut butter, and vanilla and beat until smooth.
4. In separate large bowl, mix together oats, flax, and baking powder.
5. Pour liquid mixture over dry ingredients, and mix until moistened.
6. Fold in chocolate chips and M&M's.
7. Pour into pan, press down using spoon. Bake for 20-25 minutes, until brown and springs back after touching.

Nutrition Information Per Bar

Calories 111	Fat 7 g	Fiber 2 g
Carbohydrates 12 g	Omega-3 Fats 608 mg	Calcium 26 mg
Protein 3 g	Cholesterol 13 mg	Sodium 46 mg

Moist Carrot Bars
Preparation time: 15 minutes
Baking time: 40-45 minutes
Yield: 18 bars

Joanne Shearer sends us this recipe, too. One of the wonderful things about carrots is that they are naturally sweet. If you like carrot cake, you're going to love these moist, chewy bars!

3 cups raw carrots, grated
1/2 cup brown sugar, packed
1/2 cup white sugar
1/4 cup canola oil
1/4 cup unsweetened applesauce
1/2 cup pineapple, water packed, crushed, drained
1 teaspoon vanilla
2 medium eggs
1/2 cup seedless raisins, not packed
3/4 cup whole wheat flour
1/2 cup ground flaxseed

3/4 teaspoon baking soda
1/4 teaspoon salt
2 teaspoons ground cinnamon
1/2 cup chopped walnuts

1. Preheat oven to 350 F.
2. Combine the carrots, sugars, raisins, canola oil, applesauce, pineapple, vanilla, and eggs in a large bowl.
3. In separate bowl, mix together flour, flax, baking soda, salt, and cinnamon.
4. Slowly add wet ingredients to dry ingredients and blend well.
5. Stir in chopped walnuts.
6. Coat 9 X 13 pan with non-stick spray.
7. Pour batter in pan. Bake for about 40-45 minutes or until a toothpick comes out mostly clean. DO NOT OVERBAKE.
8. Frost if desired with cream cheese frosting.
9. Nuts can be omitted from the cake and use in or on top of the frosting.

Nutrition Information Per Bar

Calories 161	Fat 7 g	Fiber 3 g
Carbohydrates 22 g	Omega-3 Fats 1454 mg	Calcium 32 mg
Protein 3 g	Cholesterol 24 mg	Sodium 103 mg

Mary Flint's Pride of Iowa Cookies
Preparation time: 15 minutes
Baking time: 8-9 minutes
Yield: 36 cookies

1 stick unsalted butter
2/3 cup brown sugar, packed
2/3 cup white sugar
2 whole eggs
1 teaspoon vanilla
1 cup all-purpose flour

1 cup ground flaxseed
1 teaspoon baking powder
1 teaspoon baking soda
1/4 teaspoon salt
1 cup quick cooking oats
1/4 cup shredded coconut
3/4 cup semi-sweet chocolate chips

1. Preheat oven to 375 F.
2. In mixing bowl, beat together butter and sugars. Add eggs and vanilla and blend in well.
3. In large bowl, mix flour, flax, baking powder, baking soda, and salt.
4. Pour liquid ingredients over dry ingredients and mix until moistened.
5. Mix in by hand oats, coconut, and chocolate chips.
6. Drop by rounded teaspoon on cookie sheet (using non-stick spray).
7. Bake for 8-9 minutes or until brown.

Nutrition Information Per Cookie

Calories 114	Fat 6 g	Fiber 2 g
Carbohydrates 14 g	Omega-3 Fats 902 mg	Calcium 25 mg
Protein 2 g	Cholesterol 19 mg	Sodium 74 mg

Rosie's Super Cookies
Preparation time: 15 minutes
Baking time: 10-12 minutes
Yield: 46 cookies

Here's another bit of bakery brilliance from my sister. When she says these are "super" cookies, she really means it!

1/2 cup (1 stick) unsalted butter
1 cup white sugar
2 whole eggs

1 teaspoon vanilla
1-1/2 cups all-purpose flour
1 cup ground flaxseed
1 teaspoon baking powder
1/4 teaspoon salt
1/4 teaspoon baking soda
2 cups quick cooking oats
1/2 cup cranraisins, dried cranberries, or raisins
1/2 cup white chocolate chips

1. Preheat oven to 375 F.
2. In mixing bowl, beat butter and sugar. Add eggs and vanilla and blend in well.
3. In separate bowl, mix flour, flaxseed, baking powder, salt, oats and baking soda.
4. Mix dry ingredients with wet ingredients until moistened.
5. Fold in cranraisins and chocolate chips.
6. Drop by rounded teaspoon on greased cookie sheet(using non-stick spray).
7. Bake for 10-12 minutes, or until the edges are brown.

Nutrition Information Per Cookie

Calories 94	Fat 4 g	Fiber 1 g
Carbohydrates 13 g	Omega-3 Fats 708 mg	Calcium 18 mg
Protein 2 g	Cholesterol 15 mg	Sodium 35 mg

Orange Walnut Flax Cake
Preparation time: 15 minutes
Baking time: 30 minutes
Yield: 8 servings

This recipe is from Chef Stephanie Green, a Registered Dietitian who hails from Phoenix, Arizona. Stephanie designed the recipe to be a quick and easy way to introduce people to the wonderful flavor of flaxseed. Please contact Stephanie if you are in her area, or check out her services on the web at www.nutritionstudio.com.

1/3 cup unsalted butter
1 cup white sugar
2 large eggs
1/2 cup fresh squeezed orange juice
1 teaspoon grated orange zest
1 cup all-purpose flour
1 cup ground flaxseed
1-1/2 teaspoons baking powder
1 teaspoon ground cinnamon
1/3 cup finely chopped, toasted walnuts

1. Preheat oven to 350 F.
2. Combine the butter and sugar in a medium mixing bowl, and beat until light and fluffy.
3. Add eggs, orange juice and zest, beating constantly.
4. Mix in dry ingredients.
5. Fold in the nuts by hand.
6. Grease a 9-inch round baking dish and line with greased parchment paper and pour in batter.
7. Bake 30 minutes or until cake springs back when touched.
8. Garnish with powdered sugar.

Nutrition Information Per Serving

Calories 353	Fat 19 g	Fiber 5 g
Carbohydrates 40 g	Omega-3 Fats 4434 mg	Calcium 110 mg
Protein 7 g	Cholesterol 74 mg	Sodium 115 mg

Harvest Pear Crisp
Preparation time: 15 minutes
Baking time: 40 minutes
Yield: 8 servings

Here's another one of Cindy Gay's contributions. I'm sure that this is a popular offering whenever it appears on the menu of the Health Sciences Center Cafeteria of the West Virginia University Hospital.

6 cups fresh sliced pears
1 tablespoon fresh lemon juice
2 tablespoons plus 2 teaspoon white sugar
1 tablespoon cornstarch
1-1/2 teaspoons ground cinnamon
1/3 cup ground flaxseed
1/4 cup brown sugar, packed
1/3 cup quick cooking oats

1. Preheat oven to 350 F.
2. Combine pears and lemon juice in a baking dish (coated with non-stick spray), toss gently to coat.
3. Combine sugar, cornstarch, and two-thirds of cinnamon; stir with a whisk.
4. Add cornstarch mixture to pear mixture; toss well to coat.
5. Mix flax, rest of cinnamon, brown sugar, and oats in separate bowl. Sprinkle evenly over pear mixture.
6. Bake for approximately 40 minutes or until pears are tender and topping is golden brown.

Nutrition Information Per Serving

Calories 157	Fat 3 g	Fiber 5 g
Carbohydrates 33 g	Omega-3 Fats 1261 mg	Calcium 39 mg
Protein 2 g	Cholesterol 0 mg	Sodium 5 mg

Pumpkin Tart with Flax Pecan Crust
Preparation time: 15 minutes
Baking time: 45 minutes
Yield: 8 servings

Crust
1/3 cup ground flax
3/4 cup quick cooking oats
3/4 cup whole wheat pastry flour or all-purpose flour
1/2 cup toasted pecans + 16 halves for garnish

1/2 teaspoon cinnamon
pinch of salt
4 tablespoons maple syrup
1/4 cup canola oil

Filling
1 cup vanilla or plain soy milk
1/4 cup tapioca
1 – 15 ounce can 100 % pure pumpkin
1/2 cup + 2 tablespoons maple syrup
1 teaspoon fresh grated ginger
2 teaspoons ground cinnamon
1/4 teaspoon salt
1/4 teaspoon ground cloves
1/2 teaspoon ground nutmeg

1. Preheat oven to 375 F, place rack in middle of oven.
2. Lightly coat with non-stick spray a 9 inch tart pan w/ removable bottom or pie plate.
3. Blend in food processor dry ingredients(except flax) to a coarse meal.
4. In separate bowl, whisk together oil and syrup, and then combine using a fork with dry ingredients, until a soft dough forms.
5. Mix in flax.
6. Press mixture into the bottom and sides of pan.
7. Bake for approximately 10 minutes.
8. In food processor, blend soy milk and tapioca until smooth, about 15 seconds.
9. Add all the other filling ingredients and process until thoroughly blended, scrape down edges as needed. (Taste filling and add spices to suit your own preferences).
10. Pour into crust –lightly jiggling it until smooth and even.
11. Bake for about 35 minutes—crust should be brown and outside inch of filling should be set. The inside will firm up as it cools
12. Decorate top with pecan halves.
13. Cool completely in refrigerator (about 3 hours) before serving.

Nutrition Information Per Serving

Calories 326	Fat 15 g	Fiber 6 g
Carbohydrates 44 g	Omega-3 Fats 2004 mg	Calcium 69 mg
Protein 6 g	Cholesterol 0 mg	Sodium 210 mg

Strawberry Cheesecake Crisp
Preparation time: 15 minutes
Baking time: 50 minutes
Yield: 8 servings

Filling
8 ounces light cream cheese
1/2 cup powdered sugar
1 teaspoon vanilla
1 egg, lightly beaten
1 teaspoon all-purpose flour

Crust/topping
2 cups quick cooking oats
1/3 cup all-purpose flour
½ cup ground flaxseed
¾ cup brown sugar, packed
3 tablespoons unsweetened applesauce
3 tablespoons chopped unsalted butter
1 cup fresh strawberries, sliced

1. Preheat oven to 350 F.
2. In bowl, mix together oats, flour, flax, and brown sugar together.
3. Add applesauce and butter pieces, and mix until crumbly.
4. Press 1 3/4 cups of mixture into pie plate(coated with non-stick spray).
5. Top with berries.
6. In food processor, blend all filling ingredients and pour over topping.

7. Evenly sprinkle with remaining topping.
8. Bake for approximately 50 minutes.

Nutrition Information Per Serving

Calories 364	Fat 15 g	Fiber 5 g
Carbohydrates 50 g	Omega-3 Fats 2035 mg	Calcium 87 mg
Protein 9 g	Cholesterol 54 mg	Sodium 105 mg

Cherry Cobbler
Preparation time: 15 minutes
Baking time: 20 minutes
Yield: 12 servings

1 pound pitted tart red cherries
1/4 cup white sugar
1 tablespoon quick-cooking tapioca

Biscuit Topping
3/4 cup all-purpose flour
1/2 cup ground flaxseed
2 tablespoons white sugar
1 ½ teaspoons baking powder
1/4 teaspoon salt
1/4 cup canola oil
1/4 cup skim milk
1 egg

1. Preheat oven to 400 F.
2. In a saucepan, combine cherries, sugar, and tapioca. Let stand for a few minutes.
3. Cook and stir till slightly thickened and bubbly, about 5 minutes. Take off heat.
4. Coat 8 1/4 X 1 3/4 inch round baking dish with non-stick cooking spray.
5. Pour cherry mixture in dish.

6. In medium bowl, combine flour, flax, sugar, baking powder, and salt.

7. Cut in oil till mixture resembles coarse crumbs.

8. In separate bowl, in combine milk and egg. Add to dry mixture; stir just to moisten.

9. Spoon biscuit topping on cherries.

10. Bake for 20-25 minutes. Serve warm.

Nutrition Information Per Serving

Calories 155	Fat 8 g	Fiber 3 g
Carbohydrates 20 g	Omega-3 Fats 1767 mg	Calcium 62 mg
Protein 3 g	Cholesterol 18 mg	Sodium 119 mg

Banana Foster Express
Preparation time: 5 minutes
Cooking time: 10 minutes
Yield: 6 servings

This one's for the seriously indulgent among us. Don't even pretend to think that this dessert isn't fattening. Still, if you exercise a little moderation, there's no reason you can't treat yourself to this once in awhile.

1 cup heavy cream
1 cup brown sugar, packed
1/2 cup rum
2 tablespoons brandy
1/8 cup banana liquor (optional)
1/4 teaspoon ground cinnamon
1/8 teaspoon ground nutmeg
1 stick unsalted butter
1 teaspoon vanilla
2 cups banana slices
1/2 cup toasted flaxseed
6 scoops vanilla ice cream

1. Cook cream and sugar together in saucepan—simmer for 3-5 minutes, until golden brown.
2. Add liquor and spices, mix in 1-2 minutes.
3. Add butter and vanilla and mix well.
4. Add banana and take off heat.
5. Fold in flaxseed.
6. Serve over ice cream.

Crepe Suzette
Preparation time: 10 minutes
Cooking time: 8 minutes
Yield: 12 crepes

Here's another sinfully indulgent recipe. Make sure you jog an extra mile or two to work off the excess calories that this dessert will to your intake!

4 tablespoons unsalted butter
1/2 cup orange juice
1/3 cup white sugar
1 teaspoon fresh lemon juice
grated zest of 1 small orange
2 tablespoons Grand Marnier
2 tablespoons Cognac
12 crepes (see below)
1/2 cup Grand Marnier

1. In a large skillet over medium heat, combine the butter, orange juice, sugar, lemon juice, and orange zest. Bring mixture to a boil, stirring to melt the sugar, then continue to boil just until slightly thickened, about 2-3 minutes.
2. Stir in Grand Marnier and Cognac.
3. Return the sauce to a boil and boil for about 30 seconds.
4. One by one, place crepe in sauce. Allow each one to heat through and soak up some of the sauce, about 15 seconds.
5. Using tongs, fold the crepe into quarters, so that it forms a ruffle-edged triangle.

6. Arrange 2 crepes on each plate so that they overlap each other slightly in the center.

7. When you are ready to serve, pour a little of the remaining sauce over the crepes.

8. Then heat Grand Marnier in a saucepan until warm and spoon over the crepes.

9. Standing well back, ignite with a long wooden match. Serve still flaming.

The Crepes:

Preparation time: 5 minutes
Cooking time: 10 minutes
Yield: 12 crepes

1/2 cup all-purpose flour
1/2 cup skim milk
1/4 cup ground flaxseed
1/3 cup lukewarm water
1/2 cup toasted flaxseed
2 whole eggs
2 tablespoons unsalted butter, melted
1-1/2 tablespoons white sugar
pinch salt

1. Combine all the ingredients in a blender or food processor until smooth.

2. Pour the batter into a pitcher or other container with a pouring lip.

3. Cover with plastic wrap and let stand for 30 minutes or refrigerator for up to 2 days.

4. Using a non-stick pan over medium heat, pour about 2 tablespoons of batter in the pan. Make sure you lift the pan off the heat and tilt and rotate it so that the batter forms an even, very thin layer.

5. Cook until the top is set and the underside is golden. Turn the crepe over, using a spatula or your fingers and cook until the second side is lightly browned.

6. Remove the crepe to a piece of wax paper.

7. Continue cooking the rest of the crepes, and stack between sheets of wax paper.

8. Use immediately or let cool, wrap airtight, and freeze up to 1 month.

Creme Brulee
Preparation time: 10 minutes
Cooking time: 1 hour and 45 minutes
Yield: 8 servings

Do you want to feel just a little bit decadent? Just a little bit wicked? This is the recipe that will do it for you.

2 cups heavy cream
3 large eggs
1/2 cup white sugar
3/4 teaspoon vanilla
1/2 cup toasted flaxseed

1. In a saucepan, heat heavy cream to a simmer.
2. In medium bowl, stir eggs and sugar together until blended.
3. Gradually stir egg/sugar mixture into heavy cream.
4. Strain through a fine-mesh sieve into a bowl or large measuring cup with a pouring lip.
5. Stir in vanilla.
6. Pour into 8 custard cups or ramekins and place in a water bath.
7. Set the pan in the oven and set oven at 250 F.
8. Bake until the custards are set but still slightly quivery in the center when shaken, about 1 top 1-1/2 hours.
9. Remove custards from water bath and let cool at room temperature.
10. Cover tightly with plastic wrap and refrigerate for at least 8 hours or up to 2 days.
11. Before serving, caramelize the surface using method below.

Caramel Glaze
2/3 cup white sugar
1/4 cup water

1. Place a bowl filled with cold water near the stove.
2. Place sugar in saucepan and drizzle water evenly over it.
3. Over medium heat, gently swirl the pan by the handle until a clear syrup forms(do not stir).
4. When syrup is clear, increase to high heat and bring to rolling boil; cover pan and boil for 2 minutes.
5. Uncover pan and cook the syrup until it begins to darken.
6. Gently swirl the pan by the handle once again and cook the syrup until it turns a deep amber.
7. Dip the bottom of the pan in cold water for 2 seconds to stop the cooking.
8. Immediately spoon a scant tablespoon of the hot caramel over each custard and tilt the mold to cover the surface evenly.
9. Refrigerate custards for at least 30 minutes up to 6 hours.

Finding Your Flax

For your recipes to end tasting spectacular, you need to start every recipe by using the highest quality flaxseed available. Throughout our journey in the flax industry, we have learned that when flax is grown, it can vary greatly with omega-3 fat content, as well as quality. Flaxseed of poor quality can contribute to having your flaxseed spoil more rapidly. It is important to select a merchant who is committed to consistently providing the best quality flaxseed available. We are very confident that any of the vendors listed below will provide you with the highest quality flaxseed, and leave your recipes tasting superb!!

North American Nutrition

We are very happy to be associated with this Minnesota company. Their golden flaxseed is grown and harvested in Canada, and they pay special attention to quality. This makes them an outstanding source for whole and ground flaxseed. To place an order, call (800) 387-5516 or visit their website, www.goldenflax.com.

Golden Valley Flax

This North Dakota family farm business is owned and operated by Mark and Esther Hylden. Mark is a fourth generation farmer, and his wife Esther is a registered nurse. Together they provide their customers with wonderful flax. To place an order, call (701) 331-1272 or visit their website, www.flaxhealth.com.

Omega-Life, Inc.

Founded in 1986, Omega-Life Inc. is a family owned business dedicated to providing the highest quality flaxseed products possible. Their pioneering spirit made them one of the first providers of flax products. Omega-Life may be contacted by calling (800) EAT-FLAX (328-3529) or log onto www.fortifiedflax.com.

Dakota Flax

MAGCO Dakota Flax™ is a three-generation family agricultural operation in Sherwood North Dakota, near the Canadian border. All Omega flaxseed available through Dakota Flax has been certified as organically grown by Farm Verified Organic (FVO). Call 701-838-2794 or visit their website at www.dakotaflax.com.

About the Authors

Jane Reinhardt-Martin, known to her clients and TV audiences as "Dietitian Jane," received her B.S. degree in Dietetics and Food Service Management from the University of Wisconsin at Madison in 1986. In that same year she was accredited as a Registered Dietitian by the Amercian Dietetic Association and the Mississippi Valley Dietetic Association. She has also been a certified Jazzercise instructor.

She has devoted her career to promoting health and fitness, and to improving public awarness about these issues. Dietitian Jane published *Flax Your Way to Better Health*, the first consumer guide on flaxseed. She also has been published in such professional journals as *Nutrition Forum and the American Journal of Clinical Nutrition*. She has appeared as a food commentator on the Paula Sands Live Show, on KWQC-TV6, and NBC affiliate out of Davenport Iowa, and has even produced a video, *Exploring Vegetarianism: A Healthy Alternative* in 1999. In addition, she serves as a consultant for area hospitals, head start agencies, and physician offices.

Ron Garrett received his Culinary Arts degree from Joliet Junior College and a B.S. degree in Hospitality Management from Florida International University. He is a Certified Executive Chef (CEC) through the American Culinary Federation and has over 25 years experience. Chef Ron is a corporate chef for a major food service distributor in the midwestern United States.

Flax Your Way to Better Health, the first-ever consumer guide on flax and nutrition. In this book, you'll learn about the long history of this "humble" seed. From Ancient Egypt to the present, people have known about the remarkable benefits that flax can bring to your daily diet, and modern science is beginning to understand just where those benefits come from.

Personally Autographed!

Flax Your Way to Better Health, $12.95 plus $1.50 Shipping and Handling. Illinois residence, add $.92 sales tax.

You can order this book directly using your credit card, through our website www.flaxrd.com. Or you can use the hand order form below. Just fill it out and send it with your check or money order to: Jane Reinhardt-Martin, 3711 23rd Avenue, PMB 158, Moline, IL 61265.

Name : _____

Address : _____

Address : _____

City: _____ State : _____ Zip: _____

Please send me _____ copies of *Flax Your Way to Better Health*.

Amount Enclosed : _____

Please add $1.00 postage for each additional copy

Please Make Autograph To : _____

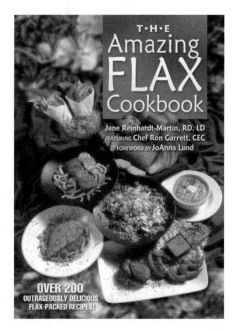

The Amazing Flax Cookbook, will show you how to incorporate this health-promoting, omega-3 rich food into your diet. You'll get easy-to-make recipes and daily menu plans designed for maximum health, and weight loss for those who need it.

Over 200 recipes including Breakfast Foods, Soups, Casseroles, Mexican Dishes, Comfort Foods, Italian Dishes, Smoothies, Main Dishes, Salads, and much more!

Personally Autographed!

The Amazing Flax Cookbook, $17.95 plus $1.75 Shipping and Handling. Illinois residence, add $1.26 sales tax.

You can order this book directly using your credit card, through our website www.flaxrd.com. Or you can use the hand order form below. Just fill it out and send it with your check or money order to: Jane Reinhardt-Martin, 3711 23rd Avenue, PMB 158, Moline, IL 61265.

Name : _____

Address : _____

Address : _____

City: _____ State : _____ Zip: _____

Please send me _____ copies of *The Amazing Flax Cookbook*.

Amount Enclosed : _____

Please add $1.00 postage for each additional copy

Please Make Autograph To : _____

Pg 214 walnut granola

Pg 5 diveriticulosis